WHEN TOLERANCE IS NO VIRTUE

Political Correctness, Multiculturalism & the Future of Truth & Justice

S. D. Gaede

Foreword by James Davison Hunter

INTERVARSITY PRESS
DOWNERS GROVE, ILLINOIS 60515

InterVarsity Press® is the book-publishing division of InterVarsity Christian Fellowship®, a student movement active on campus at hundreds of universities, colleges and schools of nursing in the United States of America, and a member movement of the International Fellowship of Evangelical Students. For information about local and regional activities, write Public Relations Dept., InterVarsity Christian Fellowship, 6400 Schroeder Rd., P.O. Box 7895, Madison, WI 53707-7895.

ISBN 0-8308-1699-2

Printed in the United States of America ∞

___

Library of Congress Cataloging-in-Publication Data

Gaede, S. D.
    When tolerance is no virtue: political correctness,
  multiculturalism & the future of truth & justice/S. D. Gaede;
  foreword by James Davison Hunter.
      p.   cm.
  Includes bibliographical references.
  ISBN 0-8308-1699-2 (alk. paper)
    1. Christianity—United States. 2. Christianity and culture.
  3. Truth (Christian theology) 4. Christianity and justice—United
  States. 5. Political correctness—United States.
  6. Multiculturalism—United States. 7. Toleration—United States.
  8. United States—Church history—20th century. 9. United States—
  Politics and government—1993-   I. Title.
  BR526.G34   1993
  261'.0973—dc20   93-41903
                                            CIP

___

15	14	13	12	11	10	9	8	7	6	5	4	3	2	1
05	04	03	02	01	00	99	98	97	96	95	94	93		

Leonard Gaede
1917-1976

in gratitude for his love of
truth and justice
and me

Foreword by James Davison Hunter _____ 9

_____

1 In These Days . . . _____ 11
  What's going on in our culture? _____ 14
  What's going on in the church? _____ 15
  How should we respond? _____ 17

_____

2 Political Correctness _____ 20
  What is PC? _____ 20
  Where did PC come from? _____ 22
  Tolerance in history _____ 24
  Tolerance today _____ 25
  Where do we stand? _____ 28

_____

3 Multiculturalism _____ 31
  What is multiculturalism? _____ 31
  Why the debate? _____ 34
  Why has this happened? _____ 38

_____

4 Understanding the Situation _____ 40
  Victims of injustice _____ 40
  Victims of relativism _____ 44
  Victims all _____ 49

_____

5 Knowing What We Believe _____ 50
  Knowing and doing what is right _____ 50
  Seeking justice _____ 53

Affirming truth _____ 56

Following Christ _____ 60

6 **Being Who We Are** _____ 62

Who makes up the church? _____ 63

What is the truth we believe? _____ 65

One God _____ 67

All have sinned _____ 68

Truth and love _____ 69

Conclusion: From whom should we take our cue? _____ 73

Appendix 1 From Truth to Tolerance:

Tracking a Change in Consciousness _____ 75

Appendix 2 Where Truth and Tolerance Endure:

A Case Study _____ 90

Notes _____ 113

Foreword

We are surrounded by clichés. By and large they sound good, and they seem to make sense out of the often confusing world around us. Even on college campuses, where one might expect a more serious and intelligent level of discussion, clichés seem to be our primary means of speaking to one another. We see them written on people's clothing, pasted on their foreheads and shouted out in temper tantrums of shallow conviction.

We should not be surprised. Clichés emerge naturally in a context where cultural norms are fragmented and contested, where the pace of life is frenzied, and where people are desperately searching for some coherence to their lives. But clichés can be dangerous.

First, they lack substance. To be sure, clichés are invoked authoritatively, as though their meaning were self-evident, by people who often seem to know what they are talking about. But the words tend to ring hollow. Why is that? Clichés do violence to nuance, subtlety and qualification. Indeed, they signal our culture's impatience with serious thought.

While clichés have little depth of meaning, they do have power. For clichés are like flags: they symbolize our political loyalties more than they communicate substantive ideas. They are a shorthand for showing whose side you are on. To question these words is to question our loyalties. This is the power of clichés: they intimidate, coerce and divide people.

Among the dominant clichés of our day, particularly on college campuses, are the words *multiculturalism, diversity, tolerance* and *political correctness.* At first these terms seem quite benign, especially to the Christian. What could possibly be wrong with tolerance? Isn't it true that Christ died for humanity in all of its diversity? Aren't we supposed to love our neighbors as ourselves? But then we confront speech codes that criminalize thoughts and words, and we see in others (and perhaps ourselves) a reluctance to speak out or to take particular positions for fear of being told we are insensitive or perhaps even intolerant. In the end, and the more one reflects on the matter, all of the talk about multiculturalism and tolerance can be pretty confusing.

In this volume, Professor Stan Gaede unpacks the bewildering controversy around multiculturalism, tolerance and political correctness with extraordinary clarity and insight. He carefully explains the origins of the terms, the meanings underneath them and why there is so much contention today. He shows that when operating within a biblical understanding of truth and justice, Christians can neither embrace nor reject these clichés outright. The higher obligations Christians live by require both a discernment and an engagement that makes genuine tolerance possible—a tolerance rooted in love and commitment rather than a tolerance rooted in indifference.

At the end of the twentieth century, we find ourselves in the midst of a culture war—a struggle to define the terms by which diverse peoples will live together. The campus is one of the chief battlegrounds for this larger conflict, and words like *multiculturalism* and *political correctness* are among the weapons wielded. Needless to say, it is partly because public discourse is dominated by clichés that the culture war rages as it does. Professor Gaede provides a foundation on which Christians can enter discussion about these important issues with intelligence and integrity. His dissection of this debate for Christians is an essential one for our time.

James Davison Hunter

1

IN
THESE
DAYS...

We live in strange times. Or the times we live in make strangers out of folks like me. I'm not sure which. That was brought home to me last summer while I was doing research at the University of California, Berkeley.

Case one. I arrived at Berkeley during the middle of the day via the Bay Area Rapid Transit System, a system that the locals complain about but that seems nearly palatial to a Bostonian. The minute I left the subway and ascended to the street, however, I was overwhelmed not only by an entirely unfamiliar aesthetic but by two distinct sounds as well. The first sound was rather tame and came from a man standing only a few feet away. He spoke out familiar words: words of repentance and salvation, words of the Bible, words of an evangelist.

The second, much louder voice came from a fellow across the street; his message was directed not at passersby like me but at the evangelist. He was in less than full agreement with the evangelist; in fact, he was heaping all manner of abuse upon the evangelist.

What struck me, however, was not the fact of his antagonism but the content. For instead of accusing the evangelist of false teaching, he accused him of false practice; instead of "Not true, not true," the chosen mantra of this accuser was "Unfair, unfair." What galled him, in other words, wasn't the fact that the evangelist proclaimed good news but that he had the audacity to proclaim bad news as well: the very bad news that sinners stand condemned by their sins and need to repent. That was unprincipled. That was unfair. That was intolerance, pure and simple, and it didn't even deserve a hearing.

Case two. There are always demonstrations going on at Berkeley, just as there is always traffic in Times Square. During my time there, the major concern was the confiscation of a portion of People's Park for the construction of a volleyball court. From the outside, of course, this is laughable. But within the dominion of Berkeley, it's serious business. And so you will not be surprised to learn that during my brief stay, there were a whole series of demonstrations and counterattacks, and that by the time I left the area, I too was convinced that world history hinged on the resolution of this issue. They must put something in the water.

What intrigued me, however, was not the brouhaha over People's Park but a second demonstration going on near the entrance of the university. I won't tell you precisely what it was about, but I will say that these demonstrators were advocates for a certain way of life—a way of life that is atypical, without doubt, but duly safeguarded under the U.S. Constitution and entitled to official protection. What intrigued me was the nature of the protest. For instead of demonstrating against some perceived legal threat to their lifestyle, the demonstration was aimed at a prominent figure in another state who had said—in public—that he thought the behavior on which their lifestyle was based is wrong.

Two things need to be noted here. First, the public figure was not talking about this particular group when he made his pronouncement. He was simply a prominent individual, living thousands of miles away, who had commented on the morality of a particular kind of behavior. Second, the demonstration was not about the truth of the public figure's claim but about *the legitimacy of making such a claim.* That is, the demonstrators argued that he had no right to make his statement in public, and that, in fact, the statement itself gave evidence that the man was deluded and obviously suffering from a profound psychosis of some sort.

Case three. The last situation occurred on the day I was leaving Berkeley and doesn't require much elaboration. Two young women—white—were walking down the sidewalk when they accidentally bumped into three other young women—Asian—walking the other way. Immediately the white women whirled around and began heaping racial insults on the Asian women, suggesting in the process that they should go back to their country of origin if they couldn't properly navigate the streets of Berkeley. The Asian women responded by asserting that America *was* their place of origin, which merely drew another round of racial epithets from the whites.

It was one of the more nauseating events of the summer, leaving me with not only a knot in my stomach but anger in my soul. And along with the first two events I've described, it left me with the conviction that we live in strange times.

What's Going On in Our Culture?

The issue raised by these incidents, I believe, is the question of tolerance in a diverse society, and the larger ethical question of how we shall relate to one another in this age. It is a question that arouses a considerable amount of debate—as these three examples suggest—because depending on where you stand, very different answers are possible.

If you are the street-corner evangelist, for example, you'd like others to give your message an open hearing, to be tolerant enough to let you speak. If you are the street-corner critic, on the other hand, you'd like the evangelist himself to be a bit more tolerant (and certainly less judgmental) about the eternal destinies of others. The same could be said of our university demonstrators, who are convinced that others ought to tolerate their lifestyle, not judge it, and who would like others to affirm the legitimacy of their way of life. But the public figure whom the demonstrators condemn also has rights, including the right to a different set of moral standards and the right to make moral judgments (in public if he so chooses). So he would no doubt like a bit of tolerance as well. And then we have our three Asian high-schoolers, who crave none of the abstract forms of tolerance the others pursue: they just want to be accepted as full-fledged members of this society and treated as such.

What we discover from all this then—not only in Berkeley but across the American landscape—is that there is considerable confusion about how we ought to live with our differences, and a cacophony of contradictory justifications for one approach as opposed to another. All appeal to the need for tolerance, but there is nothing like common agreement on what that means.

In the midst of this confusion, however, stands a united church, offering the culture an alternative vision: a vision rooted not in the turmoil of the times but the values of the kingdom . . . I'm afraid not. Too often what we find among Christians today is the same confusion, containing some biblical insights perhaps, but mostly parroting the arguments of the day.

What's Going On in the Church?
That fact became especially clear to me on my trip home from Berkeley to Boston. The first involved an in-flight conversation with a graduate student in literature at a Chicago university. She was a bright, energetic Christian who had grown up in an evangelical home and was deeply committed to working out the implications of her faith in her discipline. That task, she admitted, was difficult because there were very few Christians in her department. But one thing she knew for sure: being a Christian meant supporting those who were trying to make the literary canon more inclusive. Her witness as a Christ-follower, she argued, compelled her to fight for the rights of the oppressed, including their right to have their literary voices heard and considered. As a result, she was chairing a student committee on multiculturalism in an attempt to bring diversity to her university.

When I changed planes in Chicago, I felt as if I had changed universes as well. This time I was sitting next to a businessman from Atlanta who quickly began to describe what he thought was the number-one threat facing America today. He called it multiculturalism, but it didn't sound anything like the idea to which the Christian graduate student was committed. He described it not as an attempt to find justice, but as an effort to reduce all beliefs to the lowest common denominator and eliminate truth altogether. Since he was a Christian, he said, he was committed to truth and was therefore compelled to expose error. And that meant resisting multiculturalism at every turn: in the church, in the voting booth and in the world of business. Anything less would not be faithful to Christ.

Differing opinions among Christians are not unusual, of course. What I found interesting in these encounters was what flowed from those differences. With each of these Christian travelers I took the time to talk about my experiences at Berkeley, hoping to find some unity in our common faith and purpose. But I got nothing of the sort. I found my two companions entirely at odds with one another, sympathetic to certain protagonists of my stories and white-hot with rage toward others.

The graduate student felt some compassion for the evangelist (while disapproving of his methods), but she was unsympathetic to the "moralist," as she called him—the prominent figure who had criticized a certain lifestyle. He had a right to his opinion—which she shared—but the demonstrators had a right to their lifestyle. She said she could see why the demonstrators felt threatened by his comments, and she thought the fellow should have been more discreet. But what really angered her was the treatment of the Asian women on the streets of Berkeley. That was a sign of the times, she said. And that was what Christians needed to do something about.

The businessman was also disgusted by the treatment of the Asians. But he considered the occurrence of such racist outbursts a sad fact of life about which we can do little and about which little else needed to be said. What really galled him, and

what he did say a great deal about, was the group of demonstrators, in whom he saw arrayed all the forces of hell. First,
they were practicing sin. Second, they were trying to gain legitimacy for their practices. And finally, they were using their
constitutional rights to gain political and moral advantage.
They are the real enemies of the church, he claimed, and they
are rocks on which our culture is going to be dashed; thus
Christians need to actively support those who oppose their lifestyle.

How Should We Respond?

What does it mean to be a people of truth and justice in these
days, in these times? That I believe that is the question of the
hour. As biblical people, Christians are committed to truth and
justice. On some issues we can waffle, but on this we cannot.
We worship a God who is true. We are disciples of One who
describes himself as the way, the truth and the life. And one
of the key truths God has revealed to us in Scripture, from
beginning to end, is that he is a God of righteousness who
abhors injustice and loves to liberate the oppressed.

"What does the LORD require of you?" asks the prophet. "To
act justly and to love mercy and to walk humbly with your God"
(Mic 6:8).

But what does that mean? How are we to be a people of truth
and justice in this culture, in these days? As my two conversations on the plane indicate, on that question we seem to part
like the Red Sea. And nowhere is that division more apparent
in the church today than on the issue of multiculturalism, that
philosophy of tolerance and diversity that seems to hold such
promise for some and such horror for others.

Why is that? Why do we divide so dramatically on this key

issue of our age? Why is multiculturalism perceived as such a great danger by those whose concern is the preservation of certain truths? What makes it seem to them like a specter looming on the horizon of Western culture, threatening to undermine both truth and Western culture in a single blow? And why do other Christians, who are deeply concerned to address certain forms of injustice, see multiculturalism as the potential salvation of an oppressed people—the only sure way to deal with the evils that already permeate Western societies?

One thing is for certain: regardless of how we respond, the effects of the debate over multiculturalism are being felt throughout our society, and increasingly so. Government policies are being crafted in relation to multiculturalism, by both those who support and those who oppose it. In the business sector, personnel practices—hiring, firing, promoting—are being influenced by the multiculturalism debate; and again, influence comes from both those who favor it and those who are fighting it. In elementary and high-school education, teachers and textbooks are selected in an effort to promote or inhibit multiculturalism. And of course the media are deeply mired in the debate, alternatively presenting standards that are so white even whites can't meet them and so unrealistically multicultural that people of color can only laugh. Or cry.

The point is, whether or not we are part of the debate, we are part of the culture. And the culture is wrestling—confusedly or otherwise—with multiculturalism. The question for Christians in this culture is not, Should the Christian care? That makes as much sense as asking, Should a fish swim? If you're a fish in the ocean, you swim. If you're a Christian in this culture, you care. On that point both the graduate student and the businessman have it right.

The question is, What form should our caring take? Should we support multiculturalism or resist it? And more important, how can we be a people of truth *and* justice in a society that is increasingly confused about both, and in which both seem to be on the verge of slip-sliding away?

2

POLITICAL
CORRECTNESS

T he place to begin our search for an answer, however, is not with multiculturalism but with the current issue known as PC.

What does it mean to be *politically correct?* The phrase seems to imply that there are certain political positions that are judged to be the best or assumed to be correct. But when we dig a little deeper, it becomes apparent that politics is not at the heart of the matter: attitude is. And the core requirement of current PC thinking is that one shouldn't do or say anything that some other group might find offensive.

What Is PC?

To enter the domain of any elite college in North America these days is to be immediately confronted with a variety of things that one just doesn't do, especially in the classroom or in the presence of faculty or student leaders. Some of these are not all that different from the prohibitions we learned in Sunday school—such as not using racial slurs or stereotypes and not degrading someone on the basis of gender or ethnic heritage.

As in Sunday school, not everyone follows the rules outside of class. Demeaning behavior continues to occur on campus, especially as one gets some distance from the PC enforcers.

But PC also includes an idea that would have seemed rather odd in Sunday school: the assumption that it is good to keep silent about one's own convictions if those convictions might be deemed offensive to others. Why is that?

The overt goal of PC, most would agree, is to enforce a uniform standard of tolerance, regardless of race, gender, cultural background or sexual orientation. The problem is that the items in this list—race, gender, cultural background and sexual orientation—are not precisely parallel to each other. Though each is the basis for discrimination in our society, they involve very different kinds of issues. So the question immediately becomes: What does it mean to be tolerant *in each case?* Through the years, human beings have had great difficulty answering that question, sometimes answering it poorly, sometimes not answering it at all. PC has solved that problem, however, by simply asserting that one shouldn't do or say anything that *any* racial, gender, cultural or sexual-orientation group might find offensive. In other words, PC allows each group to define tolerance for itself.

But that raises some thorny questions of its own. First, who represents each group? Humans have an uncanny ability to disagree with one another, even within the most homogeneous groups. So whom does one choose as the authority in each group? Who gets to define the norms? Needless to say, there is no shortage of volunteers, which suggests that the PC solution isn't quite as easy, or democratic, as it seems. But second, and just as difficult, what constitutes "offensiveness"? As it turns out, people are offended not only by behavior but by words and meanings as well. If any particular group gets to determine what is offensive, then they in effect determine not only how you should act toward them but also what you may say in their presence.

What is the result of all this? *The privatization of conviction.* A good example of this process occurred at Brown University during the Gulf War. According to news reports, some students decided to fly an American flag outside their window to show their support for the troops in the Persian Gulf. Eventually, however, university officials asked them to remove the flag—not because it was destroying the ivy, not because it was placed improperly, but because they thought it might offend students who did not support government policy on the war.

Of course, the university officials had a point. Brown has a large contingent of students from all over the world, after all. And certainly a number of these students, along with many of the locals, were not happy with President Bush's conduct of the war. But note: they only had a point *if one assumes that people have a right not to be offended.* Again, the objective of PC is to avoid invading anyone's attitudinal space.

In such an environment, there is only one conviction that is deemed legitimate and worthy of public displays of passion, and that is the conviction of uniform tolerance.

Where Did PC Come From?
The source of the term *PC* itself is much debated. Some think

it was the invention of neoconservatives in an effort to put liberals on the defensive. Others think it is an entirely new term, coined to describe a wholly novel phenomenon. Both are wrong. Although the PC term is new, the idea certainly is not. In every era certain attitudes and ideas are deemed illegitimate. Every era has its heresy toward which the elite are intolerant. What is different about our era's version of PC—and historically quite odd—is that it is an intolerance of those who are assumed to be intolerant.

In the past, PC generally centered on issues that were quite substantive. The Victorians were prudish about sex because they were enthusiastic about bourgeois morality. In the fifties, many Americans were intolerant of any notion that seemed remotely "pink" (socialistic) because they assumed communism to be a major threat to their economic and political freedom. Today's PC, however, is intolerant not of substance but of intolerance itself. Thus, although the politically correct would have a great deal of difficulty agreeing on what constitutes goodness and truth, they have no trouble at all agreeing that intolerance itself is wrong. Why? Because no one deserves to be offended.

On the surface, this intolerance of intolerance is a strange thing, given its internally inconsistent character. If the worst thing you can be is intolerant, then how do you express your moral outrage? If you are intolerant of someone who is intolerant, then you have necessarily violated your own principle. But if you tolerate those who are intolerant, you keep your principle but sacrifice your responsibility to the principle. Indeed, the only person who can find consistency on this matter is the individual who is wholly committed to tolerance, to the point of being entirely apathetic. And certainly the PC environment is anything but apathetic.

Nevertheless, PC thinking makes a great deal of sense if we remember that the foundation for this kind of thinking isn't traditional thought but the modern world itself. In fact, traditional societies were prone to reverse the order entirely, favoring intolerance over tolerance. The reason is not hard to understand.

Tolerance in History

Most traditional communities were rather homogeneous. Nearly everyone spoke the same language, had the same ethnic background and affirmed the same worldview. In such communities the usual assumption is that there is value in similarity and danger in diversity. To do things the community's way is to do things "correctly." There is no distinction between morality and custom, ethics and habit. Those who deviate from custom are not simply different, they are immoral; and their behavior is a threat to the community as a whole. Under such conditions, tolerance is no virtue. It is in league with evil.

There have always been exceptions to this pattern, of course, but interestingly enough, they tend to occur in places where communal homogeneity breaks down. For example, we know that during the New Testament period there was a measure of tolerance among Mediterranean peoples of different ethnic and religious backgrounds. One can see this in the book of Acts, where in spite of persecution and the novelty of his message, the apostle Paul is able to travel extensively to different communities and get a hearing for the gospel.

But note two things about the Mediterranean world at this time. First, it was dominated by a larger power—Rome—which had an interest in maintaining order among the plurality of

religious and ethnic groups within its domain. So the tolerance
that existed was not ideal from the perspective of each particular group; it was imposed from above. Second, many of the
places where Paul was received were seaports and trading cen-
ters. Such places were atypically tolerant in the ancient world,
not out of love of neighbor but out of love of money. The business of trade required interaction with people of diverse backgrounds, and thus heterogeneity of ethnicity as well as ideology
came to be accepted. Tolerance was economically advantageous.

If we leap to our world for a moment, it is clear that we
resemble first-century Mediterranean society more than the
traditional community, and for some of the same reasons. First,
much of our world is dominated by Western political power,
either directly or indirectly. And second, the economic conditions that have arisen in the West have created an interlocking
network of relationships that depend on a measure of tolerance
for their survival; national and international commerce could
not function without tolerance.

But after this the similarity breaks down, because something
far more significant than increased trade has happened in the
modern world. Along with the economic changes that have occurred in the last century or two, there have been two other
changes, first in the way we *think,* and second in the way we
live. Each of these has had a profound impact on our appreciation of tolerance.

Tolerance Today
In the first place, confidence in truth has increasingly broken
down in the modern world. This erosion can be easily tracked
in modern philosophy, art and literature, but its intellectual
roots no doubt go back to the breakdown of the Aristotelian

synthesis. We will not play chicken-and-egg games here, though. What is important to note is that the Enlightenment project—the attempt to construct a sure foundation for human knowledge—ended in failure. Western artists announced that some years ago, and the rest of the modern world has been slowly coming to the same conclusion ever since.

Second, this erosion of confidence in truth was allied with and certainly encouraged by another erosion in the modern world: the breakdown of traditional community life. With the coming of the Industrial Revolution and its need for mobile, educated and rootless laborers, there was a corresponding decline in traditional community. There weren't enough agrarian jobs around, for one thing, and that necessitated migration to the city. Another important consequence was the development of new ways of relating to one another, not on the basis of what "is" but what "can be."

In a traditional community, one's relationships with spouse, friend and neighbor were governed by the "what is" of community. The community not only provided the context for a person's marriage but very well might have determined whom one was to marry. In the mobile society, however, we have replaced the givens of traditional community with the choices of modernity—not only the choice of whom or whether to marry but also where to live, what friends to make, how to live and what to believe.

What to believe? That's the question. We moderns have options not only in lifestyle but in life-meaning. We can choose from a smorgasbord of ideological possibilities, a variety of beliefs which are offered to us daily. Such freedom of choice is certainly liberating, but the question remains: How do we select from among all the choices? And how do we know whether our choice is the right one? The first question is the easiest, and helps account for the narcissism of our age: We choose beliefs the way we choose an entrée at a restaurant, taking whatever juicy morsel pleases our palates. This not only puts the self at the center of choice-making activity—thereby erecting a new overarching worldview, with the self playing god—but also puts great pressure on those who are trying to persuade others to adopt their beliefs. The pressure is to make one's beliefs conform to consumer demand. Yesterday's theology, after all, may not sell.

Whatever beliefs are chosen, modern men and women know that *they* have chosen them. And that brings us back to the problem of truth, which Western intellectuals have been struggling with for some time and which now must be confronted by the rest of us as well. How can modern choice-makers have confidence in the truth of any particular belief when it is not the belief they held yesterday nor the one held by their neighbor today? In other words, given all the possibilities offered by pluralism, how can any of us have confidence in our own version of truth?

We are now ready to return to the issue of tolerance and the question I posed earlier: Why do we who live in the modern world think tolerance is valuable in and of itself, even though it's impossible to live with consistently? The answer is that tolerance is a value that conforms nicely to the world we live in. Having pretty much decided that truth is not attainable, we have made tolerance of a plurality of truths a virtue. Having no truths worth defending, we have made nondefensiveness a mark of distinction.

G. K. Chesterton once observed that "tolerance is the virtue of the man without convictions," and that seems to describe modern men and women fairly accurately. Our jobs, after all, require that we interact daily with people who believe quite differently from us; it is comforting to know that our tolerance for one another's heresies is a virtue. Our daily responsibilities necessitate treating a whole host of people—the salesclerk, the cashier, the pedestrian—as automatons. How useful it is to believe that such detachment is valuable. How difficult it would be to believe that each individual is made in the image of God.

I am being heavy-handed here. But the fact is, tolerance is a very convenient virtue in a world where diversity is the norm and detachment is an economic necessity. And thus it is no surprise that the best good we can come up with—the PC we would invent—is the good of being inoffensive, keeping our convictions to ourselves and minding our own business. And if those kinds of behavior are next to godliness in our world, it's not surprising that when we feel strongly about something, it is not because we value something substantive (like truth or justice) but because we are deeply opposed to anyone else's passionate concern about something substantive.

Where Do We Stand?

All of this may suggest that Christians ought to be uniformly opposed to PC in its modern incarnation. But that would be incorrect. The fact is, there is much in our culture that we *ought* to be more tolerant of, and some of these elements are included in the current conception of PC. But it is our commitment to truth and justice that compels us to affirm such tolerance, not our commitment to the modern value of tolerance or the need to be inoffensive. And that is a crucial distinction.

For example, because I am a follower of Jesus Christ, I am deeply committed to the dignity and worth of all people, all those whom God has created in his image. And not only is it wrong to inflict injustices on people because of their race or gender, but such injustices ought to be exposed and roundly condemned. In other words, it is right to respond to prejudice and discrimination with moral indignation—which is what PC involves. Men ought to feel the potential of communal wrath when they demean women. Whites ought to worry about the consequences of discriminating against blacks.

But notice: my concern here is not that prejudice and discrimination are offensive (which they are) or might cause someone emotional distress (which they most certainly will). My concern is that prejudice and discrimination are wrong.

For that reason, I think some of the current criticisms of PC are misguided. For example, it is currently fashionable to critique PC because it threatens academic freedom. Some argue that PC discourages students from speaking their minds and inhibits professors from engaging in honest intellectual debate. Since freedom of speech and thought is at the heart of the modern university, it is argued, PC represents a threat to core values of the academy.

But that seems wrong to me. *Freedom,* in such arguments, is simply another word for tolerance. That is, such folks are merely complaining that the advocates of PC are not being true to the mantra of tolerance. And of course they aren't. They can't be. But neither can those who are committed to academic freedom, unless they too are willing to practice pure apathy—and they are not.

In fact, there is not now, nor has there ever been, anything like unconditional academic freedom. All intellectual pursuits occur within certain cultural boundaries. PC is an attempt to set up those boundaries according to the values of modernity.

Proponents of academic freedom, on the other hand, are trying to limit those boundaries, but also according to the values of modernity. What we have here, then, is an intramural dispute among those who worship the god of tolerance. And neither group is managing to be the least bit consistent.

The problem with the current approach to PC, then, is not that it limits academic freedom. The problem is that it has the wrong objective. It uplifts the value of tolerance and so requires people like me to be silent about their own convictions. But I cannot be mute about my convictions. In fact, it is precisely those convictions that committed me to truth and justice in the first place, compelling me to try to uphold the value and worth of all human beings.

Without those convictions, in other words, I have no reason to be tolerant.

3

MULTICULTURALISM

We are now ready to turn our attention to the more important issue of our age, the issue of multiculturalism. In many respects, current thinking about PC is fueled by the notion of multiculturalism. The common question is, How shall we get along with each other in the light of our differences? The PC answer is largely negative and attitudinal: Try not to be offensive to others. Multiculturalism, however, takes a more positive and directive approach, arguing that the solution to our problem lies in greater inclusiveness.

What Is Multiculturalism?

With regard to the college curriculum, James Davison Hunter summarizes the argument of multiculturalism nicely. According to multiculturalism's advocates,

> the existing curriculum is politicized by virtue of the fact
> that its principal works have been composed almost entirely
> by dead white European males. White male literary critics
> canonize white male novelists; elite white male historians
> document elite white male history; white male psychologists
> test white male sophomores; and so on. Thus, progressivists
> argue, only a small part of human experience has really been
> studied—a part intrinsically contaminated with racism, sex-
> ism, heterosexism, and imperialism. Knowledge, in a word, is
> inherently biased. The solution today, therefore, is to be more
> inclusive of different experiences, perspectives, and truths,
> particularly those that have been ignored or silenced in the
> past—the voices of women, the poor, minorities, and others
> disenfranchised from the prevailing power structures.[1]

The popularity of multiculturalism varies from place to place,
but it has had a profound impact on many campuses. Most of
America's more prestigious universities have already begun
modifying their general education requirements according to
the criteria of multiculturalism, either attempting to balance
courses on Western civilization with those focusing on non-
Western cultures or replacing them altogether with courses
emphasizing cultural diversity.

Over recent decades a whole new set of majors has also
emerged, initiated with black studies in the early seventies and
continuing with women's studies, Hispanic studies and gay
studies. The idea here is that there are certain groups that have
been excluded and that therefore require more focused scholarly
attention. But attention to the group is only one objective. The
other is to cultivate new ways of seeing: to see the world as a
feminist, as a Hispanic and so on. In this sense the goal is

substantially metaphysical: to build a new worldview. And it is this goal, more than any, that causes controversy. Critics claim that such scholars lack integrity, that they have sacrificed their scholarship to their ideology.

In the same way, traditional disciplines have themselves been transformed by multiculturalism as scholars have been encouraged to view their disciplines from the perspective of previously excluded groups. Instead of seeing American history from the perspective of Euro-Americans, for example, it is argued that one ought to understand it from the perspective of Native Americans. Instead of basing all their conclusions on data generated by white male college sophomores, social scientists are increasingly asking the question feminists have been asking for some time: Where are the women? And the answer has led not only to a more inclusive data set but often to different research conclusions and different theories.

An example from my own research is typical. During graduate school in the seventies, I was intrigued by processes of sect assimilation, especially in North America. As a result, in my dissertation research I decided to try to determine rates of assimilation among Mennonite groups in North America. On the whole, it was a fairly fruitful research effort, generating not only a successful dissertation but a number of journal articles as well. But here's the interesting thing in retrospect: I studied only males. Not one Mennonite woman was included in my data set. At the time I thought nothing of this omission, since it was standard practice among sociologists. But today I believe it was a mistake of monumental proportions—and I have come to this realization only through the influence of women in my discipline.

Multiculturalism has had an impact outside of academia as

well. Many businesses and government organizations are actively trying to sensitize their employees to the needs of a multicultural environment. Such institutions often sponsor workshops that take employees through a series of experiences designed to encourage sensitivity and respect for women, minorities and people from diverse cultures—in other words, to make white males aware that they are not the only game in town.

The multicultural perspective is also being worked into public educational programs, not only in secondary education but in elementary and middle schools as well. These programs include new textbooks for all children, enrichment programs for selected students, workshops for teachers and a variety of other mechanisms aimed at making early education less male and less white. Columbus Day isn't what it used to be. Children of all ages are encouraged to think of what the *Pinta*, the *Niña* and the *Santa Maria* meant not only to Europeans but to Native Americans as well.

Why the Debate?
And what has been the reaction to these developments? Extraordinary conflict and debate. Campuses in turmoil. Faculty involved in bitter disputes. Political organizations launched for the sole purpose of initiating or preventing the spread of multiculturalism. And the list goes on.

Some of this conflict is purely political, of course. Some folks oppose multiculturalism out of a desire to hold on to power and maintain the status quo; they find a ready audience among majority-group members who fear change. Others are promoting multiculturalism for political reasons, finding that it is an easy way to mobilize alienated segments of the population and promote their own political ambitions in the process. But any caring Christian can give another reason why the conflict abounds: multiculturalism provokes as much internal conflict as external.

There is much within the agenda of multiculturalism that most Christians—and I among them—would want to affirm. Surely those who have been excluded from the decision-making process because of gender or race ought to be included. Surely those of us who are to be marked with the love of Christ—who are to be known for our peculiar love for one another and for our neighbors—ought to applaud efforts aimed at increasing our knowledge of and sensitivity to others. How can we care for another and *not* want knowledge of his or her experience and culture? And surely those who are committed to seeing the world through the eyes of Christ will not be satisfied with a selective, narrow view of history or any other discipline. Any understanding of American history that ignores the perspective of the African or the Native American peoples, for example, is simply not much of an understanding. And hardly a Christian one.

In other words, there is much in multiculturalism that seems to be a genuine response to injustice. We live in a society that has systematically disenfranchised people simply because of who they are or where they were born. The histories of Native Americans and African-Americans provide the most apparent examples, but similar tales can be told about other non-Northern European peoples, as well as women, and the story continues to this day. To be sure, we are not the only ones to have acted this way. Indeed, one could argue that such behavior is standard stuff for human beings. But the sins of others are no excuse for one's own. And by the standards of our *own* culture, we ought to have known better in the past, and we should be doing better at present. Christians should not be shy about pointing this out and siding with those who are in the right.

But multiculturalism also carries much baggage that ought to worry Christians. This baggage has less to do with the details of multiculturalism than with its general orientation. And perhaps the best way to get at this is to notice that more and more, those who favor multiculturalism argue not on the basis of a desire for justice but on the basis of multiculturalism's practical necessity or its validity as a general worldview. Let's look at both arguments.

The primary reason many businesses and educational institutions are embracing multiculturalism these days is not idealism but pragmatism. For all their high-minded talk, the reason Harvard and IBM are affirming multiculturalism is that they are increasingly dealing with racial, cultural and gender diversity in the workplace and the classroom. White males are no longer the norm in many places, and they will be less so in the future. And this growing diversity represents a potential threat to productivity. If people don't get along with one another—if some feel devalued or excluded, if managers or teachers can't communicate—then efficiency will plummet and organizational objectives won't be realized. Embracing the concept of multiculturalism, then, is seen as a way to foster more esprit de corps in the workplace and to strengthen the bottom line.

Is this a bad thing? No, in many ways it has very positive benefits. I have participated in "multicultural workshops," and I think it is fair to say that they do increase worker sensitivity and promote better relationships. Nevertheless, because they are not rooted in assumptions about what is good and right and true, they inevitably confuse the means with the ends and often turn means and ends entirely on their heads.

Christians aren't sensitive to others simply because it's good to be sensitive; we are sensitive so that we can better love others and do what is just and right in God's eyes. But this implies that our primary goal isn't being sensitive, it's promoting love, justice and truth. Sensitivity is a means, not an end. You will note, for example, that Jesus is hardly a nice fellow on all occasions, hardly Mr. Sensitive when talking with the Pharisees and teachers of the law. Why? Because he didn't understand them? Certainly not. He understood them all too well, and in his desire to promote truth and justice he spoke to them in very strong terms.

The problem with the pragmatic approach to multicultural sensitivity, then, is that it rules out Jesus' approach. It says that the end is cooperation, good relations, harmony and agreement. And it thereby undermines and displaces the true ends of human existence.

This problem only looms larger when we turn our attention to the arguments of those who embrace multiculturalism philosophically. With few exceptions, multiculturalism is not argued today on the basis of promoting justice but on the grounds of inclusiveness. And the fundamental assumption is that it is good to be tolerant of different ideas and different perspectives. In other words, undergirding current thought on multiculturalism is not some sense of what is ultimately just and true, but a very deep moral and ontological relativism. Thus the argument for multiculturalism typically runs like this: Because all cultural perspectives are equally valid, every idea or perspective ought to included. Indeed, to be exclusive about truth (to assert that one can distinguish between truth and error) is bad, while to be inclusive of all truth claims is good.

The raison d'être of multiculturalism becomes tolerance.

For this reason, it is no surprise that college course requirements in Western culture are being replaced by courses on
cultural diversity. But it would be a surprise if one had some
concept of truth. That is, if the faculty believed in truth, and
if they heard that courses in Western civilization were presenting erroneous or prejudicial material, what would be the logical
thing to do? The reasonable response would be for the faculty
to investigate the charges thoroughly to find out the truth of
the matter, after which they would take a course of action based
on the truth.

But no university's faculty could or would do such a thing
today. Instead, the faculty argue for a year or so, after which
they ask some of their members to put together a course on
cultural diversity. Why? Because as a group the faculty can't
get anywhere close to a consensus on what is true or just. The
best they can do is simply present a smorgasbord of ideas, all
assumed to be of equal value (even if inconsistent), and let the
students choose.

Why Has This Happened?

Why is it that people argue for multiculturalism on the basis
of tolerance rather justice? Because it would be fruitless to do
otherwise. Our entire culture is like the university faculty: we
simply do not know what justice means. Or we each have our
own pet notions of what justice means, which produces the
same result.

Justice has become an empty concept, a meaningless term. To
be understood, justice requires a moral foundation. To determine what is just, one must have a rather clear idea about what
is right and wrong. No such clear idea exists, however, and so

the advocates of multiculturalism have no choice but to root their cause in other soil.

And what is that other soil? It is the ground of tolerance and inclusiveness. For while it is impossible to know what justice means in a relativistic age, it is very easy to support the idea—if not the reality—of tolerance.

4

UNDERSTANDING
THE SITUATION

S o what do we do? We seem to be confronted with a concept that is teeming with good intentions but that is being embraced to enhance the bottom line and that is being argued according to the categories of a relativistic age. How should we respond?

My proposal is threefold: First, we need to understand the situation we face. Second, we must know what it is we believe. And third, we need to be who we are.

Victims of Injustice

I said before that we live in a culture that has consistently excluded and oppressed certain people simply because of who they are. I realize that this is a controversial assertion, even among Christians who care deeply about justice. Certainly, facts can be marshaled for and against my statement. But I am increasingly convinced that the controversy has more to do with limited knowledge than with the nature of the facts.

For that reason, arguing about the facts is unfruitful, but living in the midst of them is often life-changing. Christians who doubt the reality of prejudice or the impact of unjust discrimination must do one thing before they argue about the facts: they need to sit down with poor Christians of non-European descent and stay for a spell. Better yet, live for a spell. Why? Not because we want to be sensitive, but because we want to know the truth. These folks are our brothers and sisters in Christ. They are trustworthy. They have lived the life that we are arguing about. Why would we want to start our inquiry anywhere else?

If you were in Iraq and heard that the Kurdish people were being treated badly, where would you look to discover the truth? Certainly you would not ask Saddam Hussein. Nor would you drive to a middle-class neighborhood in Baghdad and attempt to find your answer among the Muslims living there. Why? Because though they may be fine folks, they don't have access to the information you need. Instead, you would make your way to the alleged victims and find out for yourself what was going on among the Kurdish people. There you would listen. You would investigate. And you would draw your own conclusions.

Too often, when the question of injustice comes up in this culture, we middle-class Christians do what we would find unthinkable anywhere else: we seek our answers in our own backyards, often from those who do not even share our worldview. Why would we want to do that? Why talk to middle-class Muslims in Baghdad when you can talk to the Kurdish people themselves? Why talk with middle-class Americans in your neighborhood when you can talk with family members—fellow Christians—who are among the alleged victims? That might not be the end of your investigation, but it certainly ought to be the start.

And where will your inquiry lead? Well, you will want to draw your own conclusions. But I'll be frank about my own. I think people of color—and particularly the urban poor—face extraordinary challenges in Western culture. For one thing, they have inherited a legacy of institutional racism. Slavery, broken treaties, immigration policies, disfranchisement all testify not only to past sins but to the fact that our institutions were originally designed with overt discrimination in mind. Second, institutions spring from cultures; and while overt institutional racism has been greatly reduced in the West, the culture that produced it remains. Of course, the culture too has changed. But many of the assumptions have not. As a result, minorities continue to find themselves on the short end of hiring practices, educational opportunities, business networks, health care, judicial processes and so on. In short, we have made progress on overt discriminatory practices, but covert discrimination remains highly problematic—and far more pervasive than middle-class whites assume.

One consequence is that there is a wide gulf today between what the majority group assumes and what the victim experiences. If you are a young black male living in an American city, for example, you will be routinely pulled over by the police on suspicion. You will be followed and watched closely in stores. You will be arbitrarily denied loans, apartments, jobs. And you will be conscious of your blackness every time you watch television, read the newspaper, look in the mirror. And yet your white counterpart, who has never experienced anything like this, will assume that your situation is pretty much like his—perhaps better, given affirmative action quotas. As a result, he expects you to succeed and be grateful for what your country has done for you. And you expect not to succeed, and you know precisely what your country has done for you. Both reach their conclusions based on experience, but the conclusions couldn't be more different.

Out of such experiences comes not only misunderstanding but deep resentment and anger as well. Anger that is born of injustice, on the one hand, but that is totally incomprehensible to the majority group, on the other.

It is precisely this juxtaposition of righteous indignation and ignorance that makes multiculturalism so attractive. Victims know that they are being treated unfairly. They do not need a discourse on justice, they need action. Multiculturalism promises action—action that certainly appears to move in the direction of justice. Thus the victim does not think of multiculturalism as an end, but as a means to a more just society.

At the same time, the victim perceives the benefits of the majority group's adoption of multiculturalism. Understanding the meaning of injustice in their own lives, they know good and well that unfettered tolerance of all beliefs is a bogus concept. (What kind of parents would raise their children to be open to any and all beliefs and experiences?) But tolerance is infinitely superior to the intolerance and ignorance that they have been the victims of for umpteen years. And so—politics being a matter of compromise anyway—they accept it as a necessary trade-off. For the promise of inclusion, they'll give up on the concept of truth. No one expects to *really* have to give up on truth, of course, since you can go on believing whatever you want anyway. Until the day you try to teach it to your children and discover that it doesn't compute.

The point is, there are many victims of injustice in our society, and they are not just the poor or people of color. And among all these victims, multiculturalism is perceived as a viable alternative to the status quo. When victims listen to the debate over multiculturalism, they do not hear it with the same ears as the dominant majority. They do not hear relativism, truthlessness, accommodation. Rather, they hear change, the possibility of justice, the end of intolerance. And that is an attractive outcome, especially when there are no better ideas on the table.

Victims of Relativism

Yet injustice is not the only problem that plagues our culture. Indeed, one could make the case that the problems of injustice are themselves a *moral* problem, rooted in what we believe and value. When victims hear such words these days, a red flag goes up, because "moral problem" can be a code word for blaming the victim (for example, insisting that the conditions of the poor are due to their own moral failings). But I'm not talking about the moral failings of the victims, I'm talking about the moral breakdown of a culture as a whole—and especially of those who provide intellectual leadership.

I was frank in my characterization of injustice, so let me be equally forthcoming here: We live in a culture that is riddled with moral and ontological relativism. In the first place, most of us would have a hard time articulating what we believe. Moreover, what we believe today is easily displaced by something else tomorrow. Our beliefs are more a matter of feelings than anything, and thus our confidence in them varies with our hormones, our situation and our friends. Most important, our beliefs are *our* beliefs, and that, we think, makes them worthy and beyond dispute.

Relativism (moral, not descriptive) is the idea that all values and beliefs are equally legitimate and that you cannot judge between them. By "equal" I mean not equal before the law but equal before the barrister of truth. Thus you may believe in God and I may believe in Zippy the Clown. Before the law we both have the right to hold our different beliefs, and there is nothing necessarily relativistic about such equality. But if one were to say that each belief had equal value—that my belief in Zippy was just as true as your belief in God, and there was no way to arbitrate between them—then one would be making a relativistic claim (which, interestingly, can't be argued on its own grounds).

One of the consequences of this form of relativism is that it is increasingly considered inappropriate to try to change someone else's mind. My experience with the evangelist in Berkeley is only one example, but increasingly, every evangelist feels the power of relativism. These days it is a scary thing to stand face to face with another person and suggest that their ideas may be wrong. So we try to be as indirect as possible, laying out the gospel message in a way that will sound attractive to the modern ear. Even then, however, it is scary business. Sit down with a group of evangelicals these days and you will discover that they are petrified to express their faith. How odd, we may think, since they live in a society where such freedom is protected by law. But their reticence is not odd at all when we consider that one of our culture's deepest values is tolerance, and that value is embedded in a relativistic worldview. To assert truth in such an environment is blasphemy. Evangelists are the heretics of our age.

But the values of relativism are not merely "out there." They are in us—certainly within me. One of the things I have noticed about myself, for example, is that I am more inclined to react to speakers' style than to their content. If they speak politely and in a self-effacing manner, if they use self-deprecating humor and seem open to the opinions of others, I react positively even if their teaching is flawed. On the other hand, if they are strident or abrasive, if they appear to be absolutely confident of their position, I don't like them regardless of their position. Why? Because deep in my gut I care less about truth than about style. Viscerally at least, I'm a relativist.

I'm not alone. Two years ago I was speaking at a conference of evangelicals. The keynote address was delivered by a well-known figure, a major rider on the evangelical circuit. As is almost always the case, he was well received. People laughed. People were moved. And when he finished, he was given a standing ovation. There was only one problem. According to what Christians have believed for almost two thousand years, he was not speaking the truth. Many non-Christians have shared his convictions, however, and—over the years—it has not been all that difficult for Christians to figure that out. But it is difficult for us in our age—even those of us who claim to be the heirs of the orthodox tradition. Why? Because we care far more about how speakers make us feel than what they say. Again, style over content.

But why do we moderns find relativism so attractive? If my argument in chapter two holds, we find it appealing for both philosophical and sociological reasons: we have lost both the *grounds* for believing in truth and the *communities* necessary to cultivate and transmit truth from one generation to the next. Consequently, relativism has more plausibility for us—it makes more intuitive sense—than even the mildest forms of dogmatism.

Given that fact, it might be helpful to remind ourselves of relativism's effects. What's the problem with relativism? I will mention only three.

First, in the short run, relativism undermines the credibility of any form of orthodox belief. By "orthodoxy" I do not mean only Christian doctrine but any belief in a historical body of truth, whether contained in Torah, the Koran or the Bible. Relativism says, "You have your beliefs and I have mine, and that's just splendid." Orthodoxy says, "Truth exists, whether we believe it or not, and believing falsely is anything but splendid." The problem is, orthodoxy always appears intolerant in a relativistic culture. In my experience, Christians want to be nice. But how can you be nice when your basic beliefs are an offense to the deepest values of an age? And so there is tremendous pressure on the orthodox to mend their ways, to bend their beliefs to modernity in order to make them more acceptable.

In the long run, however, all beliefs are thrown into question by relativism. That is especially the case in an individualistic culture such as our own. It is one thing to practice "communal relativism," which says that each community's beliefs are equally legitimate. It is quite another to say—as we do—that each individual's beliefs are equally valid. In the former, at least people can be held accountable to the standards of their own community. In an *individualistic* relativist culture, however, there can be no accountability, except the accountability of brute force. Why? Because there is no basis for saying whose ideas are right. All are equally legitimate. So whoever has the most votes, or the most power, or the biggest guns, decides what's right. Might makes right.

And that leads us to the second problem of relativism: it

makes the good society impossible. This may seem an odd claim, since most of us are inclined to equate tolerance with the good society; and relativism promotes tolerance and thus helps achieve that end. But as we have already seen, relativism's end result is not tolerance but rule by power—not most people's idea of the best of times.

A more standard (and even a minimal) definition of the good society would be one that cultivates people of virtue: people who treat each other fairly, who act wisely, who have the courage to do what is right and who practice restraint and self-control. But how can one cultivate any of those things in a relativistic setting? Why practice self-control if truth is up for grabs? What need is there for courage to do what is right, when whatever I believe at the moment is right? What reason is there to pursue wisdom when there is no larger body of truth out there to pursue? How can I treat others fairly if there is no standard—and why would I want to? Why not treat them merely as a means to an end, the end being my own good pleasure?

Finally—and perhaps, most importantly—relativism makes the doing of justice impossible. Justice requires a moral foundation. That is why it is so closely linked with the concept of *righteousness* in the Bible. To do justice, one must know the difference between right and wrong.

This is rather obvious—so much so that I hesitate to bring it up—yet it is routinely denied in our age. We moderns like to say, for example, that law is not about morality but the establishment of rules to minimize harm. So, it might be argued, we have laws against rape but not pornography, because the former does physical harm but the latter is a matter of personal morality. But such thinking breaks down almost immediately. What do we mean by "harm," and who gets to define it? No doubt there are some rapists who deny they are doing harm, and many women who think pornography is immensely harmful. But we have passed laws that deny these definitions of harm. Why? Because those who make laws believe some definitions of harm and not others; that is, they have established what they think is a *right* definition of harm.

There is no getting around the relationship between justice and some moral code. But we like to hide that fact these days, because we cannot agree on a moral foundation and affirm relativism at the same time. If everyone's ideas are okay, then no idea is right. And so we deny the need for such a foundation of *right*ness and hope against hope that we can build a decent society undergirded by relativism. For that reason we promote multiculturalism—not as an effort to establish justice based on some moral vision, but simply to achieve indiscriminate inclusion. But what we end up with instead is not tolerance, nor inclusion, and certainly not justice. What we get is Robespierre: people with power deciding what is best for all and executing their will accordingly.

Victims All

The point of this chapter, then, is very simple: We live in a society that is victimized by both injustice and relativism. We like to think of these as different problems, and we even pit seekers of truth and justice against one another, but we do so only because we have allowed relativism to define the problem for us. For those seeking justice, relativism seems like a friend, but it comes at the cost of truth. For those seeking truth, relativism is clearly the enemy, but it seems to come at the cost of justice.

But there is no truth without justice, no justice without truth. Only victims without the slightest hope of finding either.

5

KNOWING
WHAT
WE BELIEVE

Understanding the situation, then, is our first need. If we ignore it, not only will we misconstrue the issues in which the current struggle is rooted, but we will not be able to act wisely. But just as important, and just as easily ignored, is the second need: Christians must know what they believe. Not merely in the head, but in the gut, in the heart.

Knowing and Doing What Is Right

The apostle Paul concludes his letter to the Ephesians with these familiar words: "Finally, be strong in the Lord and in his mighty power. Put on the full armor of God so that you can take your stand against the devil's schemes" (Eph 6:10-11). And what does the armor of God consist of? "Stand firm then, with the belt of truth buckled around your waist, with the breastplate of righteousness in place, and with your feet fitted with the readiness that comes from the gospel of peace" (vv. 14-15). Paul continues the metaphor by calling Christians to take up also the shield of faith and the helmet of salvation—two armaments that evangelicals readily acknowledge and try to cultivate. Of faith and salvation we know a great deal.

But what about righteousness and truth? Why does Paul start with these? And why does the apostle assume that they are so important in the battle against evil?

The answer is no mystery: There is no fighting evil without them. Without truth we cannot distinguish between good and evil. And without righteousness we will not have the gumption or resources to carry out the fight.

Evil is cagey. It is both the great deceiver and the great tempter. Like the serpent in the Garden, it first undermines the truth ("you will not surely die"—Gen 3:4) and then lures us with attractive possibilities ("you will be like God"—Gen 3:5). Without the armaments of truth and righteousness we will neither recognize evil's lies nor resist its invitation.

That insight is especially important as we come to the topic of multiculturalism. As we have seen, in the debate that surrounds multiculturalism both sides seem eager to employ half-truths to serve their cause, and motives are mixed at best. In the midst of such confusion and temptations, Christians need to clearly understand what is true and what is right.

Moreover, the debate over multiculturalism almost always attempts to separate truth from justice. But Christians cannot afford to give in to such a false dichotomy. We worship a God who is just *and* true. Whose word can be trusted. Who shows himself to be deeply offended and moved by injustice. And who has, and is, and will be bringing his righteousness and justice to this world. If we are not on the side of both truth and justice, we are not on God's side.

To some extent this is simply a modern version of the old debate between knowing and doing: does being a Christian mean that one knows that Jesus is the Christ, or that one lives as if he is the Christ? But what a silly debate this is in the light of the Bible's own understanding of those words! From Scripture's perspective, to know is to do. When Abraham *knew* Sarah, they both believed and acted, and together they *conceived* a nation. When Peter, James and John began to get a glimpse of who Jesus really was, they followed him and became his disciples. The authenticity of the knowing is demonstrated in the actions. Even the demons believe. The point is, real understanding leads to changed behavior.

Again, this is an obvious point, made difficult by the times in which we live. We live in a world that not only separates knowing from doing but increasingly considers that normal. We see this in the home, where families routinely watch the evening news and yawn. We see it in the classroom, where students see no relationship between what they learn and how they ought to live. We see it in the church, where Christians find it easy to affirm certain beliefs but then live as if they didn't matter. We have become knowledge consumers, not responsible knowers. As a result, we think of learning as a head game more than a serious undertaking, and we tend to value discussions of truth over its application.

Such an approach to knowing ought to be deeply troubling to Christians. Certainly it was troubling to Jesus. Have you ever noticed who it was that provoked Jesus' anger? Time after time, it was the Pharisees, the teachers of the law, the scribes. Why? We tend to think it was because they were Jesus' primary intellectual adversaries. But the Pharisees were theologically closer to Jesus than most other groups were. What disturbed Jesus was that they knew the truth but didn't practice it. Indeed, they used the law to lift themselves up and to put heavy burdens on others. They were hypocrites, in other words, employing their knowledge for their own benefit and not living out the implications of what they knew to be true.

Seeking Justice

Our world, then—and specifically the debate over multiculturalism—attempts to drive a wedge between knowing and doing, truth and justice. And Christians must start with Christ's assumption that such thinking is deeply and fundamentally flawed. It is not biblical. It is not possible. And it is not right. Using Paul's language in his letter to the Ephesians, we ought to consider the wedge one of the devil's schemes, against which we will need to be armed by the belt of truth and the breastplate of righteousness.

But what are the implications of that truth as we confront the issues raised by multiculturalism? First, it means that we are on the side of justice and—for that reason—sympathetic and responsive to the concerns that give rise to multiculturalism. Christians cannot turn a blind eye to the problems of prejudice, racism and exploitation that exist in our society. We cannot wink at such evils, nor can we simply accept them as the inevitable consequences of human fallenness. No caring parents would do that in their home. Why would we think it acceptable elsewhere? Christians, like the God whom they worship, must love righteousness and seek justice—in their homes as well as their neighborhoods, communities, nation and world.

And yet that's a worry, isn't it? Time and time again, I have

discovered that when Christians are confronted with the necessity of doing justice, they admit to the need but worry about the
results. The reasons usually come down to two. In the first
place, they think the requirement to pursue justice implies a
certain political affiliation. They assume that if they are encouraged to care about justice, they are actually being urged to join
a particular party or take up a particular political cause. And
they worry that they are being subtly coaxed into accepting
someone else's agenda, an agenda that they may have real reser-
vations about.

It is important to say, right from the start, that we must
distinguish the Christian's responsibility to seek justice from
the question of political affiliation. Christians have disagreed
dramatically over the years on the right way to engage themselves politically. What we must not do is allow such disagreements to undermine our common commitment to justice. That
assumption precedes affiliation. If you are a Christian, you care
about justice. The political question—how can we best act upon
that assumption in the public arena?—is a secondary question
about which Christians can and will legitimately disagree.

This does not mean that the secondary question is unimportant, by the way, which leads me to the other reason Christians
often balk at the need for justice: they see the need in wholly
personal terms. If I were to say that it is important for a parent
to promote justice and fair play in the home, few Christians
would quibble. But when we move beyond the hearth—to the
neighborhood, community, economy or nation—Christians do
quibble, quite strongly at times. Why is that? Good question,
since it is difficult to find even a few verses in Scripture that
might remotely justify such a distinction. The Bible speaks of
doing justice, period, and it gives examples involving neighbors,

nations and businesses as well as family.

The reason we limit the question of justice to individual and family behavior, then, doesn't have much to do with the Bible but does have a great deal to do with our culture. We live in an individualistic culture, one that values individuals more than communities. As a result we defend individual rights, not community rights, and we tend to think of our responsibilities in very personal terms. Thus Christians in our culture may think long and hard about what it means to be a good parent, but they won't often ponder what it means to be a good citizen or to have a just society. Those might seem like interesting questions to us, but they don't seem particularly relevant to our faith.

One consequence of this is that Christians, by default, wind up duplicating the politics of their peers rather than developing political positions that reflect their commitment to justice. For example, studies have consistently shown that North American Christians tend to "vote their occupation." That is, if you know their occupation—along with their region, class and educational background—you can pretty closely predict how they will vote. And that's troubling, because it means that most Christians are not voting to promote justice, they are voting to protect their pocketbook or other interests, just like everyone else. And they aren't doing this because they're callous or mean-spirited, but because they've never thought as carefully about the implications of seeking justice in the nation as they have about seeking justice in their own family.

Again, the point here is not to endorse any particular political vision. Rather, it is to make clear that the issues of justice are every Christian's concern, regardless of whether they involve the family, business, neighborhood, or nation. If you, as a parent, adopted children who were black and brown and white, you would be very careful to not only treat them all with equal respect, but to make sure that an environment was established which encouraged your children to treat one another that way as well. In other words, you would actively promote justice in your home. Can we do any less in our neighborhoods, businesses, and nation?

For the Christian, the answer is clearly no. For regardless of what we think about the concept of multiculturalism, we know what we think about the concept of justice. And we know we'd better be doing it. Indeed, according to Jesus, for those who know the truth, the only other option is hypocrisy.

Affirming Truth

That is, of course, unless we give up on truth altogether—a possibility that the Pharisees wouldn't have considered, but that almost seems to make sense in our own culture. A culture bent on "knowledge consumption" and "irresponsible knowing" breeds hypocrisy. It specializes in it. And where hypocrisy reigns, cynicism and skepticism are not far behind. For hypocrisy undermines the truth it pretends to support. Cynics understand this and take delight in revealing the hypocrite's pretensions. They proclaim boldly what the hypocrite believes underneath: that the truth is a lie. Metaphysically, the cynic and the hypocrite share the same assumptions.

The problem is, the modern world makes a life of integrity— a life without hypocrisy—extremely difficult. Consider the day of a typical university student—let's call him Steve. At 8:00 he takes a shower while talking to his roommate about the keg party the night before. At 8:30 he has breakfast with a Hare Krishna devotee who not only didn't attend the party but doesn't even drink Coke. At 9:00 he attends an ecology class where the predominant assumption is that humankind and nature are one. Later at the library, he begins work on a research paper exploring a neo-Marxist interpretation of the fall of the Soviet empire; afterwards he meets his girlfriend for lunch and conversation, the overriding theme of which is how the two of them feel about one another. In the afternoon he attends a lecture on macroeconomics that offers an entirely different interpretation of the Soviet collapse; this is followed by a quick dash to the lounge so he can catch another installment of *As the World Turns*.

Which is not a bad title for Steve's life, or for ours. In any given day, modern college students will find themselves swept into a wide variety of discrete frames of reference. But students are not alone in this experience. We all spend our days moving in and out of conversations, turning from one set of assumptions to the next. And in each conversation we adjust to the new reality, acting as if the current set of assumptions were *the* reality. We reminisce about the party as if existentialism were true, we write the paper as if Marxism were true, we talk to our lover as if romanticism were true, we watch the soap as if nothing were true. And of course, when we lie down on our beds at night, that's exactly the conclusion our daylong exercise in fragmentation has led us to: it's all a sham, a pretense. And so deep down in our gut we become cynics and skeptics, distrustful of anyone who believes anything, assuming that the believer is merely someone who is even more hypocritical than we.

In such an environment it is not easy to be people of truth. In the first place, it is not easy to live a life of integrity based on truth. And in the second, it is difficult for those who do seek integrity to resist playing the cynic, both to demonstrate to the world their "honesty" and to avoid being associated with hypocrites themselves. And yet that is precisely what Christians are called to do, in this age or any other. We are on the side of truth not because it is easy, but because it is right. And we cannot play the cynic in order to make ourselves appear truthful, any more than we can sin in order to appear sinless.

As people of truth, then, Christians must resist the twin temptations of hypocrisy and cynicism, because both undermine the truth. But equally undermining of the concept of truth is the notion that "all truths are equal," an idea especially tempting to Christians concerned about multicultural justice. Its attraction lies in the fact that it appears to be an egalitarian approach to cultural differences that also assumes the existence of truth. In this way it seems to offer the Christian a way of believing in truth while respecting the beliefs of others at the same time.

The problem, however, is that this assumption—which is really a form of relativism—immediately turns into nonsense the minute we investigate any particular truth claim. If Mary claims that God is the sovereign Lord over history and John believes that God is the ineffable Force of *Star Wars,* in what sense are both claims true? Certainly Mary and John may agree on certain divine attributes, but their basic beliefs are distinctly different.

The question is, how can we do justice to both John's and Mary's truth claims? Relativism's answer is that we ought to assume that they are both true, that they both give us insights into a larger truth. That sounds nice on the surface, but to accept this interpretation one has to deny the essential validity of *both* truth claims. In other words, what relativism requires is the conclusion that both claims are flawed and that relativism itself is the larger, grander truth. By asserting that all truths are equal, it actually denies the validity of a good many truth claims. And in that sense, it is not nearly as tolerant as it purports to be and certainly doesn't do justice to a great many beliefs.

I would argue that we respect our differences more authentically by taking each truth claim seriously on its own terms. That means recognizing differences where they exist, not attempting to gloss over them, but considering them points at which learning may take place. After all, one or both truth claims might be entirely false. And the recognition of error, or its potential, is perhaps the single most important step toward human understanding and wisdom. Certainly we do ourselves—and those with whom we disagree—no favor by denying our differences and covering them up with a philosophy that is both nonsensical and undermining.

Christians are not relativists, and we have no reason to apologize for that fact. We believe in truth. For that reason, we ought to honor our honest differences with others (and among ourselves) by recognizing them and seeking understanding. The assumption that truth exists, after all, frees us from fearing differences and from ignoring the differences that exist.

It's important to realize that bigotry and hatred toward those who are different from us do not stem from a genuine confidence in truth. Quite the reverse. Only those who are confident about truth can have the assurance that truth will prevail. They know that truth does not hinge on them, nor will it be lost if they happen to lose an argument. Intolerance of differences comes from those whose confidence in truth is shaky, who think truth depends on them. Thus it is not the genuine truth lover we ought to fear, but those whose love of truth is not genuine. And that includes the hypocrite and the cynic as well as the relativist.

Following Christ

The point, then, is that Christians are lovers of truth *and* justice. We cannot decide between the two, because they are inextricably tied up with one another. As we approach the issue of how we shall live with our differences, therefore, we must remember: We are inclusive of people but not of beliefs. We ought to listen and learn from all people, but we will not agree with all people. We will embrace the speaker but not the spoken lie.

Our model in this task, of course, is Jesus Christ. Like us, he lived in a world of differences, a world where bigotry and hatred and injustice ran rampant. And how did he respond? His approach to the Samaritan women at the well was typical. In talking with her, he crossed all kinds of cultural boundaries. He was a man who shouldn't have been talking with a woman. He was a Jew who shouldn't have been involved with a Samaritan. He was a religious teacher—a rabbi—who shouldn't have been seen with a "sinner." Yet he crossed all these barriers to talk with her, to include her in his world.

And what did he say to this woman to whom he reached out, and on whose behalf he had broken all the conventional prejudices? I'm okay and you're okay? All truths are equal? No. First he asked her for water, which was not only an entrée for a discussion of "living water" but a physical demonstration of his willingness to commune with her. Second, he told her the truth, that she had had five husbands, not one, and that she was living in adultery. For Jesus knew what was true, and he acted on that truth. He knew she was a human being created in the image of God. He knew she was a sinner in need of forgiveness and restoration. And he loved her.

What strikes me is that what Jesus did in this situation is

precisely what few would do in our own culture. Our inclination is to be either unabashedly inclusive or exclusive: we would have either rejected her totally or affirmed her every word. But Jesus would have none of that. Loving justice, he did not let prejudice prevent him from doing what was right. Loving truth, he did not let the situation prevent him from saying what was true. Loving the woman, he did not let the world prevent him from acting on the basis of that love.

Can those who claim Jesus as their Lord do any less?

6

BEING WHO WE ARE

C hristians who arm themselves with truth and righteousness will not necessarily come to the same conclusions, even if they are committed to common principles and have a good grasp of the situation. To some extent that's as it should be. We are finite beings, living in a complex, fallen world. We can't know every relevant fact, nor see the whole picture; our insights and conclusions will vary with our circumstances. Indeed, such diversity is actually a strength if it operates under a unity of purpose, for it improves our collective judgments and enables the Christian community to act with greater wisdom.

But sometimes our disagreements reflect not wisdom, but a misunderstanding of who we are. So as we think about the issues raised by multiculturalism and draw our conclusions, it might be helpful to keep two questions in mind: Of whom is the church constituted? And in what truth do we believe?

Who Makes Up the Church?

It is certainly understandable that when we think of the church universal, we tend to think of the people in our local church. They are the people who make up our church experience, after all. They are the flesh and blood that gives concrete meaning to our understanding of the body of Christ.

Still, this is a dangerous tendency when we are thinking about the issue of differences. And it is, in fact, quite wrong. The real church is—and always has been—multicultural. Jesus started the multicultural church when he crossed religious, gender and ethnic lines in order to heal and teach. The early church picked right up on that theme when they discovered that the Holy Spirit was indwelling converted Gentiles as well as Jews. And within a few decades the good news had spread east and west, making inroads into highly diverse cultures and people.

Of course, I misstate the case. Actually, it was God who made his church multicultural, and it was his intention from the beginning that it be so.

It is terribly important that Christians today remember that fact, and that we develop a mental image of the church that corresponds to reality. When we think of the church we must conjure up a picture not of people like ourselves, but of people of all colors and shapes and ages, women and men speaking different tongues, following different customs, practicing different habits, but all worshiping the same Lord. Having such a concept is important because that *is* the church. It is important because that is the church that Jesus sees. And it's important because that is the church that Christ has called to represent his kingdom on earth. We do ourselves and Jesus a great disservice when we think otherwise.

If our image of the church is wrong, we also set ourselves up for poor thinking about the issues of multiculturalism. For regardless of what we conclude about the pros and cons of that particular ideology, we ought to *feel* multicultural in our bones. The church is multicultural. Our brothers and sisters in Christ—those who are our family in the truest sense of the term—come from a wide variety of backgrounds. And that is a striking thing, isn't it? Jesus made it quite clear that at times he would come between biological family members—that he would divide brothers and sisters, parents and children. But he would also form a new family, made up of his disciples, and they would become his church. Its members are our true brothers and sisters. They are the people with whom we have the most in common. They are the people with whom we will spend eternity. And they are multicultural.

What this means, I think, is that not only do we need to regularly remind ourselves of who we are, but we need to structure our lives to reflect that reality. Church behavior in North America is odd in one way. On the one hand, we live in a society that contains a very diverse population of Christians; on the other, we go to church with people who are pretty much like us.

The reasons for this are many and hotly debated. Two of the most significant involve the way we think about church and the way we live. First, we tend to think of church as a voluntary association, which we select according to our own needs; thus we choose churches containing people with whom we can identify and whom we enjoy—people who are like us. Second, we live in neighborhoods stratified by class and race; thus white middle-class Christians tend to live in white middle-class neighborhoods. In such a situation, the local church often turns out to be white middle-class as well.

Regardless of why this takes place, it presents a multicultural church with a problem: the local church reflects neither the diversity of the church universal nor the reality of the church in our own society. We are isolated from one another in the body, and that breeds misunderstanding, ignorance and an inaccurate picture of the church.

The question is, how can we deal with and learn from our differences if we don't ever see or commune with Christians who are different from us? The answer is, we can't. And so I believe one of the central tasks of the church in the decade ahead must be not only to figure out ways to overcome our isolation but also to work together to confront the issues of living in a multicultural society.

To be sure, given our history, this will be no easy task. But it seems to me that we have no choice. If the church won't do this, who will? And if the church can't accomplish this, who can? Or perhaps it's more accurate to put it this way: If the church can't do it, how can it in fact be the church?

What Is the Truth We Believe?

As we confront the question of differences, then, we need to remember that we are members of the church, and the church is multicultural. But we also need to remember that the truth we believe is not without definition or content. Though Christians affirm truth, they don't do so because truth is a nice philosophical concept. Rather, we affirm truth because we believe some things *are* true.

Every so often I find myself engaged in discussions where this fact seems to get lost. In the first chapter I described two such conversations—those I had on board a flight from Berkeley to Boston. The businessman from Atlanta clearly defined himself as a defender of truth; and in some ways he was. But what was the truth he was defending? Was it the truth of the gospel, or was it truth as it has come to be understood in his culture? And was he upset about multiculturalism because it threatens the gospel or because it threatens the political status quo? To some extent that's an unfair question, I know; truth always comes to us via culture, and it is impossible at times to distinguish what is "gospel truth" from cultural details. Yet there are differences. One of the ways we sort out those differences is by watching Jesus and seeing what it means to live according to the truth. And I wasn't sure I saw Jesus in this man's words or posture.

I wasn't sure about the graduate student either, to be honest. Certainly she demonstrated care and commitment for the oppressed; and in that way she was speaking Christ's language. But there were other things that worried me. Her commitment to multiculturalism, for example, seemed to be unrestrained and almost indistinguishable from her commitment to Christ. I began to wonder whether it was an expression of her faith or whether her faith had become multiculturalism itself, into which she was bound and determined to fit the teachings of Christ. In this way she had something in common with the businessman: both were wholly committed to a particular ideology about multiculturalism, out of which they interpreted the teachings of Scripture. Consequently, neither was able to see the potential pitfalls in his or her own position. And both came very close to replacing God with the ideologies, or idols, of our age.

So I think it is very important not merely to defend truth but to remember the core truths that Christians believe. Let me mention three that have special significance for the issue of multiculturalism.

One God

First, *there is one God, Creator of all, and we are all created in his image.* Many of us have come to be embarrassed by this claim, but we should not be. It is the basis of a universal understanding of the human family. Remember, before the Hebrews there was plenty of pluralism; it said you have your god and I have mine, and my god can beat up your god any day of the week. The typical conclusion was that superior gods produced superior people, and superior people had the right and duty to oppress those who followed inferior gods.

God told the Hebrews, however, that there was only one God, and that all people were his creations. He chose the Hebrews not because they were great, but precisely the opposite: they were a ragtag band of nobodies in the eyes of the world, through whom God was going to demonstrate his power and purpose. But the point of the demonstration was who God was, not who the Hebrews were. What was most important was that God is One and that all people are his image bearers.

This truth makes all people our brothers and sisters—whether they agree with us or not—and deserving of respect and dignity. In the past, Jews and Christians may have practiced bigotry and racism and even rationalized it using certain scriptural texts. But anyone who has read Genesis with a clear head—and especially anyone who has compared it with other creation stories—knows this for certain: the Bible is remarkable in the extent to which it shows human beings to be alike, with the same God, the same problem and the same need. That is the point of Adam: he is the father of us all. And that's the point of Eve's being "flesh of his flesh": she is of the same substance as Adam, and mother of us all.

What does this mean for our relationships with others? When we meet others who are different from us, our very first inner response should be "Here is my sister, my brother, bearing the very image of God." I do not overstate the case when I say that the full realization of that fact would revolutionize human relationships. *Cf. Newton Jewish Story*
Behold the image of God.

All Have Sinned

Second, we all have the same problem: *all have sinned and come short of the glory of God.* Again, we sometimes find this assumption embarrassing, because we have been told that it is not a particularly nice thing to say about others. But we don't say it about others; we say it about *everyone,* most especially ourselves! Christians do not assume that others have a problem; we assume that we all have a problem. There is no basis for pride in the doctrine of sin; we have all missed the mark.

This awareness does two things: it provides us with a healthy skepticism and a healthy humility. In the first place, our universal problem should make us leery of any arguments that focus entirely on one particular problem. For example, arguments that assume multiculturalism is *the* problem or that it is *the* solution both miss the mark, because neither assumption accounts for sin's pervasive and intractable character. Such assumptions are naive. And Christians should be the least gullible people in the world. We ought not to be surprised by sin; and we ought not to assume that any single solution will entirely resolve the problem. That doesn't mean we stop trying, of course; the fact that your children are sinners doesn't mean you stop training them. Training makes a difference. But a parent also knows that training isn't the whole story, that children make choices. And wise parents are anything but gullible.

Our underlying assumption about sin should also give us a healthy humility. One thing I have never understood is the existence of arrogant Christians. I find that a contradiction in terms. How can we, who understand our own poverty before God and his grace in our life, have even a stitch of arrogance? Recognizing your own sin doesn't make you feel superior, it makes you weep and seek mercy. And when you receive forgiveness, you are overjoyed and deeply humbled. The one thing you can't possibly feel is superior or arrogant.

I find it particularly disturbing, therefore, when we discover arrogance among those who are supposedly teaching the truth—professors like myself as well as preachers, missionaries and church leaders of all types. How can the core truth that we are sinners be taught in anything but deep humility? Of course it can't. Which means that those who teach this truth out of arrogance aren't teaching the truth at all.

Recognizing our sin, then, doesn't separate us from others, it joins us to one another—in our common predicament and our need for the grace of Christ. As the story of our creation requires that we treat each other with dignity and respect, the story of the Fall is the basis for humility regarding ourselves and compassion toward others.

Truth and Love

Third, *Jesus Christ is the Truth, and the Truth calls us to love God and love others as ourselves.* Here we come to the nub of the matter: What is true, and what does the truth require of us?

John puts it like this: "In the beginning was the Word, and the Word was with God, and the Word was God. . . . The Word became flesh and made his dwelling among us" (Jn 1:1, 14). Jesus Christ is the embodiment of truth, because he is the incarnation of God in human form. Those who wish to know what it means to live in truth will need to pay attention to him.

And what does the truth require? That we love God and love others as ourselves—precisely what the Old Testament prophets said, and indeed a summation of the divine law given to Israel. So we have in this command a bottom-line ethic, a foundational truth. Christians are to be known for their love. It is our mark of authenticity. "Let us not love with words or tongue but with actions and in truth. This then is how we know we belong to the truth" (1 Jn 3:18-19).

It seems to me that this connection between truth and love is especially vital as we confront the issue of our differences. Each side of the current debate over multiculturalism would have us separate love and truth. Advocates of exclusion often do so as protectors of truth, while advocates of inclusion place themselves on the side of love. But actually the two are inseparable. It is the truth that calls us to love; and it is our love that testifies to the truth.

But what does this love entail? First, it calls us to love God. And that means, among other things, listening to his Word. Enjoying his creation. Obeying his commands. Appreciating his gifts. Following his directions. Acting according to his will. Having our hearts set in tune with his. Honoring him with our gifts. Doing what is right. Forgiving others as he has forgiven us. Being good stewards of his world. Loving justice. Doing mercy. Walking in humility.

And it also means loving others as we love ourselves, for the second part of the command is inseparable from the first. Indeed, the primary way we know of someone's love for God is by their love for others. That's why love is the one distinguishing mark of a true follower of Christ. Everything else in the above list can be faked. Like the Pharisees, you can enumerate in detail the requirements of the law and live your life in a way that seems to be holy, just and righteous. But you cannot fake the command to love others as you love yourself. Either you do it or you don't.

And so it turns out that the people of truth are not those who are good with words, but those who are good with actions. Those who only defend the truth with words and don't act in love are a noisy gong, a clanging cymbal. Their words are worthless, because they lie with their deeds. And followers of Christ should be just as disgusted with such duplicity as Jesus was.

Let me be blunt: Leaders and teachers in the church who do not act in love should not be endured; they should be replaced. They maintain their authority not by God's will but by their craft with words and their ability to instill fear in the hearts of others. Churches today are full of such folks, and they typically present themselves as defenders of the truth. But in fact they are destroying truth. The same goes for the critics and advocates of multiculturalism: if their deeds bear no love, their words are not worth bearing either.

To act in love, however, we must know what love entails. And again, Jesus is quite clear: he says, "Love your neighbor *as yourself*" (Lk 10:27). We act in love when we care for others as we would care for ourselves. It is too bad that this clear meaning has been obscured by the modern tendency to think of love almost exclusively as a feeling or emotional state. Love can and should result in feelings of affection, but that's not the primary meaning here. This is a command. And commands assume that those who hear the command can, and should, change their behavior. You cannot command someone to have a feeling. It doesn't work. But you can ask someone to care for another human being, whether they feel close to each other or not.

Nor is this a command aimed at how we ought to feel about ourselves. That too is a modern obfuscation that not only confuses love with feelings but also misunderstands the intent of the text. If I were leaving home for a few days and you agreed to take care of my children, I might tell you to love them as you love your own children. Wouldn't we think it odd if you then proceeded to shower *your* children with love because that's what I told you to do? The command was about *my* children, and your love for your own children was simply a benchmark for how I had hoped you would treat my children.

In the same way, Jesus is here assuming that people typically look out for their own self-interest; they take care of themselves, making sure they get food and rest and whatever else they need for daily sustenance and nourishment. The *command* is that we care for others with the same kind of concern and nurture that we typically lavish upon ourselves.

The command to love, then—and this is often a surprise to modern readers—is very closely linked with the biblical concept of justice. For one of the ways we find out whether a situation is just is to put ourselves in the place of another and *then* ask if the rules are being applied in such a way that justice is being done: if we lived in an urban ghetto or on a family farm; if we were an unborn child, or a black male, or a Korean shopowner; if we were the victim of spouse abuse, or of a drunk driver, or of an ill-prepared teacher.

The command to love others as ourselves also gives the lie to those who think that Christian love is a matter of sappy sentimentality that always gives in to the perceived needs of others. Your child, whom you love, wants all the candy she can eat. Do you give it to her? No, because you love her. You also confront her when she does something wrong; you hold her accountable. Why? Because that is how you would like to be treated if you were she. In the same way, as we love one another in the church, in the neighborhood or wherever, we will confront one another and hold each other accountable. Not because we enjoy confrontation, but because that's what we would want others to do for us.

As I noted earlier, Jesus did not engage in much sappy sentimentality; his love sometimes made him angry, and it did not prevent him from saying some very harsh words to the Pharisees. Nevertheless, it was indeed love.

The point? The truth that we believe calls us, above all else, to love. There can be no such thing as a Christian who advocates truth in the name of hate. Like justice, love is something Christians must be actively pursuing if they want to claim Christ as their Lord.

Critics of multiculturalism and defenders alike will not be judged as much by their words as by their actions. Are they promoting justice? Are their actions intended to care for others as much as they care for themselves? These are the questions of the hour. For these are the questions of Jesus.

Conclusion: From Whom Should We Take Our Cue?
And it is Jesus from whom we will need to take our cue, in these days and the days to come.

One thing is certain: the modern world does not know how

to deal with the issue of differences. It doesn't have the categories to do so. And so it vacillates between a blind affirmation of differences and an equally blind affirmation of similarities, looking to policies of inclusion or exclusion to save us. But they will not save us. Only Jesus saves. And it is only as we take our cue from him, and build our policies on the truth that he has given us, that we will be able to serve a very needy world.

Come, let us love one another, in Spirit and in truth.

Appendix 1
From Truth to Tolerance:
Tracking a Change in Consciousness

As I indicated in chapters two and three, the value of tolerance in modern societies is an odd value, historically speaking, and a complicating factor for Christians who are committed to both truth and justice. It might be useful, therefore, to consider two questions in greater depth. First, why is it that tolerance has assumed the value of an end—a virtue—in modern societies? And second, is it possible to have a society where a deep commitment to truth is assumed but where people practice tolerance nevertheless? Here and in the appendix that follows, I will explore both of these questions—in this chapter by tracking the modernization process in the West and focusing on its effect on truth, and in the next by investigating an unusual historical case of truth and tolerance. In both chapters my concern is not with tolerance in the broadest sense, but with what might be called ontological tolerance—that is, tolerance of those who hold very different notions of ultimate truth.

It should be noted that neither of these chapters is necessary to the argument I set up in the main body of this book; they are explanatory, not definitive, intended for readers who wish to explore these issues in more depth. For the same reason, the arguments here are somewhat more complicated and the prose slightly less friendly. Nevertheless, jargon has been kept to a minimum, and I have attempted to make these sections as readable as possible. For the historically and sociologically curious, I think both appendixes will be accessible. I trust they will be helpful as well.

A Case of Tolerance

Let's begin by considering the story of the Pilgrims.[1] Except this time, instead of starting the story with their landing on Cape Cod, let's begin in England, where the Puritans are trying to practice their faith but having a very difficult time of it. After much deliberation, they finally resolve to escape persecution by fleeing not to America but to Holland, that redeemed bit of lowland across the channel. And amazingly enough, in Holland they get precisely what they sought, the freedom to practice their faith without threat to life or limb.

But here the story turns interesting, especially to those of us in the modern world. For soon we discover that the Pilgrims become dissatisfied with their new home, not because they are once again the victims of intolerance, but precisely the reverse. In Holland they are confronted with a new but equally burdensome difficulty, the problem of tolerance. A tolerance that threatens not only their way of life but their religious faith as well. The Pilgrims, you see, are becoming Dutch, seduced by the charms of a tolerant, accepting culture.

And so they decide to escape to the New World. Not to avoid religious persecution, as we typically assume, but to avoid assimilation into an alien culture.

This means that the Pilgrims' objective in the New World was not precisely "religious freedom"—at least not as we have come to employ that term. The freedom they were seeking was the freedom to establish their own way of life, rooted in the particularities of their faith and culminating in a distinctive society. In other words, it was not the freedom to be unencumbered individuals, picking and choosing from a smorgasbord of religious and cultural options. Rather, they wanted the freedom to establish a community of faith, unhindered by the requirements of other religious faiths. They sought the freedom to establish their own dogma.

That fact, I believe, has led to a rather mixed picture of the Pilgrims in our own era. On the one hand we have the children's story which pictures them as lovers of liberty, willing to risk their lives in order to find religious freedom. Later, however, we are forced to add the rest of the narrative; and suddenly the Pilgrims are transformed into uncompromising Puritans, rigid in the application of their faith and intolerant of the religious proclivities of others.[2] In fact, however, the Pilgrims were neither lovers of liberty nor religious imperialists, but people who sought the freedom to be a people of faith—a community. They did not seek freedom for freedom's sake, but for the sake of truth. For that reason, both the intolerance in England and the tolerance of Holland were a problem for these Puritans. Committed to truth, they wanted the freedom to practice it. Committed to truth, they were not willing to compromise it in the name of freedom.

Truth and Tolerance

This is not a plug for the Pilgrims, nor a defense of the theology they wished to protect. But one does suspect that the Pilgrims had a far more perceptive understanding of the relationship between truth and tolerance than most of us living in the modern world. That suspicion is based not so much on the superiority of their intellectual life—though one could make a fairly strong case for that—as on the nature of their circumstances. Unlike most of us, the Pilgrims were saturated with the idea that their religious faith was a manifestation of truth. Not truth in the midst of truths, as we moderns might put it. But truth in the midst of error.

That assumption, however, placed the Pilgrims in something of a bind—a bind that gave them a better vantage point from which to view the issue of tolerance. On the one hand, it confronted them daily with the problem of intolerance. Their understanding of truth was a minority opinion. It was not the dominant view of the day, and thus they fell victim to persecution, abuse and ridicule. More problematic, because those holding the dominant position were equally convinced of the veracity of their own beliefs, the Pilgrims were the victims of coercion—attempts to get them to change their beliefs.

The point, of course, is that the Pilgrims had an existential understanding of the consequences of intolerance. They understood the burden of the heretic.

But they were equally convinced that the heresy was not their own, that their position was that of truth. Consequently, when they set out for Holland, they were not looking simply for freedom from intolerance; they were looking for a place to put their truth into practice. Holland was a problem for them not because it lacked the requisite freedom, but because it

lacked an environment conducive to the cultivation of truth. No
doubt this judgment was rooted in a latent form of English
ethnocentrism, which preferred an English Puritanism to
whatever might sprout up in Dutch gardens. But what is clear
is that although they found tolerance in Holland, they were not
satisfied. Indeed, they found Dutch tolerance just as threatening as the intolerance of England had been. For it too imperiled
the truth—this time not by coercion, but by the poisoning effects of a polluted soil.

Still, the Pilgrims' response to Holland is something of a
puzzle to us, is it not? We understand why they left England,
certainly, but why would they wish to leave Holland as well?
Why would they want to leave tolerance behind? We scratch
our heads on this question for one reason and one reason only:
we moderns don't value truth as highly as they did.[3] This does
not mean that moderns deny the possibility of truth, and certainly it does not mean that moderns are without beliefs or
faith. Beliefs we have in abundance. But modern beliefs are
more like hunches or hopes than truths. Indeed, we make quite
a hubbub about separating beliefs from truths: we place beliefs
in the sphere of religion (read "unknown") and truths—if they
exist—in the domain of the empirical. If there are truths, then,
moderns assume that they are far removed from the transcendent and extremely focused (on the level of $E = mc^2$ or "the cat
is white")—and, of course, the best students of science and
philosophy don't believe those either.[4]

Truth as a known commodity, attainable and worthy of pursuit, is not a pervasive influence in the modern world. This is
the case not only at the core of modernity, where we might
expect to find skepticism, but on the periphery as well. Fun-
damentalists no less than secularists are far more likely to talk

about feelings and experiences than they are about truth.[5] This makes life easy for those who value tolerance, since it is not difficult to be tolerant of your neighbor's heresy if that heresy is just another belief. But it makes dogmatists difficult to stomach, and it makes people who risk all for the sake of truth (such as the Pilgrims) difficult to understand.[6] Risk to protect something valuable we readily accept. Risk to defend family or friend we view as noble. But giving up comfort and security so that we and our children's children might cherish the truth and build our lives around it? That we find more than a bit baffling.

The Idea of Truth

The important question, of course, is why this change in consciousness has come about. Why did the Pilgrims see tolerance as a potential problem while we see it as an unimpeachable virtue? And why is their commitment to truth so difficult for us to comprehend? In chapter two I gave a partial answer to this question, arguing that modern pluralism makes tolerance both necessary and attractive.[7] But pluralism always has a context. And to find a more complete answer, we must turn our attention to the context for this new perspective.

Though it is somewhat simplistic to do so, one could talk about this transformation of consciousness in relation to the two great revolutions of the modern era, the French Revolution and the Industrial Revolution.[8] The former symbolizes an ideological change while the latter has to do with change at a socioeconomic level. Both changes had their roots in prior events, including the Reformation, the Renaissance and the Middle Ages, but both were cataclysmic enough that one could describe them as decisive in and of themselves. More important for this discussion, embracing the importance of both revolutions helps us avoid the tendency to reduce the issue to either a matter of ideas or a matter of material conditions; it clearly involves both.[9]

The first, or ideological, development has sometimes been described as an assault on truth; but while that is an understandable description in hindsight, it is also substantially misleading. The changes that brought us to our current state were motivated not by a lower view of truth but, if anything, by a *higher* regard for it. If we begin somewhat arbitrarily with the Reformation, we see a series of Reformers whose primary concern was to extricate biblical truth from certain social and ecclesiastical encumbrances and thereby allow the biblical canon to speak more clearly to the general population. They were, almost to a person, deeply concerned with truth and indeed interpreted their own actions as elevating truth above its human vessels.[10] Nevertheless, in so doing they also dislodged biblical truth from its immediate tradition and democratized accessibility. Thus, epistemologically speaking, truth no longer required a particular communal tradition to be understood.

The Enlightenment took that thinking even further. Much further. For now we see truth being separated not only from a particular tradition but from any tradition whatsoever. Instead, it was conceived as sourceless, as existing out there, accessible to the reasonable inquirer. Again, this was thought of as an elevation of the importance of truth, and certainly it shows a heightened confidence that truth can be known. Moreover, many early Enlightenment thinkers did not conceive of this shift as endangering the core truths of their own tradition. Locke, for example, assumed that a reasonable inquirer would come to affirm the truths of the Christian faith, that there was total compatibility between objective truth and biblical truth.[11] Nevertheless, this conceptual change did two important things:

first, it conceived of truth as independent of community, and second, it made each individual the captain of his or her own ship of truth. Truth, in other words, was now democratized with a vengeance.

The fruit of this is more than apparent by the time we arrive at the French Revolution. On the one hand, there was tremendous optimism concerning what freethinking individuals can construct, not only politically but socially and religiously as well. Indeed, it was such optimism that made a revolution not only reasonable but necessary.[12] On the other hand, once the revolution occurred, it was nearly impossible to extract from such freethinking individuals the kind of consensus necessary to govern and reconstruct society. And again, the problem was not just political. Philosophically, the Enlightenment seemed to spin off theories in all directions, some profoundly individualistic and others communalistic, some antagonistically secular and others mystically transcendental. Each of these spinoffs arrived with great acclaim and full of possibilities, but each turned out in hindsight to be something of a fad, a naive probe into the unknown.

Questions were raised about the Enlightenment project from the beginning, but these took on added significance as the consensus failed to materialize. Central was the question of truth, most starkly unearthed in the German tradition, but evident generally in Western thought.[13] The question is: Can human beings really know anything with certainty at all? Again, the motivations of those who raised that question were numerous— some sought liberation and others confirmation, some asked it out of great angst and others out of sheer chutzpah. But the question itself was irrepressible once truth was freed from its contextual maternity, first the womb of the church and then the umbilical cord of the canon. If truth is out there for individuals to grasp through the eye of reason, why aren't they grasping it? Or, more correctly, why is every foundation for truth so readily shown to be without justification? Why can't the answers stand up to the questions?[14]

The pain of this line of inquiry has been felt differently in various sectors of society, with philosophy and the arts picking it up quite early and the hard sciences coming to terms with it only in the twentieth century.[15] But it was there at the birth of the Enlightenment, and it came on like gangbusters in the aftermath of wars, depressions and all manner of intellectual and social upheavals.

What this means, then, is that at the same time that tolerance was being given added significance as a protector of truth in an increasingly heterogeneous society, there was an eroding confidence in the existence of the truth it was protecting. But that is not the whole of the story. And in fact, as it stands the picture painted so far is somewhat misleading. For it is conceivable that the entire Enlightenment project would have evolved differently—either developing in a more uniform manner or, perhaps, never really flourishing at all—had there not been a second revolution in the making, one grounded less in philosophy and more in social and economic developments.

The Context for Truth

The demise of truth was not simply an intellectual exercise. It was profoundly influenced by the Industrial Revolution. Again, I want to emphasize that the process I am describing here cannot be understood as a simple march of ideas through history, nor were the ideas purely the byproduct of social and economic changes. As I describe the impact of the Industrial

Revolution, then, I am in no sense denying the influence of ideology on the process. Indeed, industrialization itself is a product of certain conceptual understandings which, in turn, have meaning because they rest in a particular social context. Separating the development of ideas from conditions may be a useful heuristic device, but the result ought not to be confused with reality.

The beginnings of the Industrial Revolution were immensely complicated, and current interpretations are enmeshed in a host of controversies. For the time being, though, I would like to sidestep the question of beginnings and simply take its effects as our point of departure.[16] And if we do that, a few obvious consequences immediately arrest our attention. There is, for one thing, a great population shift from rural to urban areas. This shift gives evidence to a second feature of industrialized societies: they contain increasingly mobile populations, moving not only from the country to the city but from city to city as well. Third, technological innovations require new relationships, not just with the productive forces but with people as well; thus one is more likely not only to engage in new forms of labor (moving from farm to factory, for example) but also to work with new faces (moving from family to competency-based colleagues). Finally, in this new labor environment different values become salient, including the values of efficiency, abstraction, goal-directedness and individual achievement.[17]

Even this cursory and selective overview is enough to demonstrate the mammoth changes wrought by the Industrial Revolution. But even these changes are misleadingly pedestrian if we fail to see the effects they had on the thinking processes of modern men and women.[18] I will mention only two. First, the changes that occurred in residency patterns and work requirements not only altered relationships considerably, but in fact completely redefined the meaning of relationships. Most important, they gave individuals new power over relationships, an authority we simply take for granted today.

Prior to the Industrial Revolution, relationships were part of one's taken-for-granted world. Family, neighbor, community— all these relationships were simply givens, to be enjoyed or endured as the case might be. With the advent of the mobile society, relationships were suddenly transformed into matters of individual discretion, things one chose on the basis of other needs and requirements. This, of course, represented tremendous individual liberation, since it meant that one was not stuck with any particular neighbor or friend or lover; one could build a whole new life if one wanted to. But it also changed forever the nature of community. For now the community could not simply impose its values and norms upon compliant subjects but had to woo them instead. Community was no longer valuable in and of itself, in other words; its value rested in its functional utility to individual consumers.[19]

Second, with this change in the meaning of relationships there also came a radical transformation in the locus of traditions within the community. In preindustrial societies, traditions were the vehicles by which communities wielded their power. They were the tangible representations of community life, binding one generation with another and choreographing much of communal life.[20] Thus not only did traditions define the meaning of marriage and family and work, but it was via tradition that one found one's spouse, related to one's parents and siblings, and discovered one's work. As communities lost their givenness, however, traditions lost their power as well. The initial impact of this change was behavioral: tradition played less of a role in the determination of one's spouse or work, being replaced by individual choice (which, in turn, was highly constrained by the new realities of class). The long-term effect, however, and the one that concerns us here, is that with this loss of power, tradition was no longer able to supply meaning to these institutions. Thus, now one's marriage is not the culmination of the work of divine forces but the simple product of individual choice. Marriage loses much of its ontological legitimation, therefore, unless a new, individualistic mythology can be supplied (and even then the mythology is under the jurisdiction of the individual chooser).[21]

The impact of the decline of community and tradition on truth is difficult to overestimate. Sociologically speaking, truth is conceived and nurtured within community. We learn what is true from community (family, neighbor, church and so on), and we judge the legitimacy of a belief on the basis of its communal efficacy. This is not to say that what we learn is true in some metaphysical sense, nor is it to deny that truth transcends community (as well as any sociological explanation of it). But community is the carrier of truth, and tradition supplies it with substance, fleshing it out in everyday life. When community loses its power over individual decision-making, its ability to transfer truth from one soul to another is correspondingly diminished; its judgments are immediately subject to the "who says?" of individual predilection.

When traditions no longer celebrate communal truths and no longer are allowed to provide them with meaning or symbolic value, truth is reduced to a matter of personal discretion, useful to justify individual wants and choices perhaps, but hardly a matter of eternal significance. In short, truth becomes relative to its individual host.

Conclusion: The Rise of Tolerance

What we have in the modern world, then, is truth losing its epistemological credibility at precisely the time that its sociological foundation is being transformed. This process, moreover, is taking place in concert with one other development already discussed in chapter two: increased ideological heterogeneity, or pluralism. Clearly, the coexistence of these phenomena is no mere coincidence, however. And we are now in a position to see that the epistemological, sociological and ideological changes occurring in the modern world are in no sense independent of one another. Sociological individuation, for example, exacerbates truth's epistemological problems at the same time that it promotes pluralization. Conversely, by separating truth from context, the Enlightenment not only empowers the individual to be his or her own truth bearer but also justifies individual decision-making over against communal authority; thus it supplies an ideological basis for the mobility necessary in an industrializing society and increases the probability of the pluralization of worldviews.

From all of this, one conclusion seems nearly inescapable: tolerance has not achieved its newfound status in the modern world simply on its own merits. It is not, in other words, merely the concoction of a few humanists at the Sorbonne, nor is it the consequence of a latter-day political conspiracy in Washington, D.C. Though there any number of worldviews that support its modern incarnation, it holds its position in large part because the truth that it was once summoned to protect no longer seems worth protecting.

What this suggests, among other things, is that those who decry its present influence in the hopes of bringing about some quick-and-easy change, though quite possibly well-meaning, are

nurturing a vain hope. Any attempt to deal with the problem
of tolerance must first appreciate the fact that it is fundamentally a problem of truth. Tolerance cannot even be understood
or conceived of as a problem in the first place (as our Pilgrims
did) unless one holds dear some measure of truth. And tolerance
will not be put in its place unless truth is assumed to be the
greater value.

Our discussion also indicates, however, that the linchpin
issue in recovering any sense of truth is the problem of community. We will not cultivate truth-seeking citizens in a society
bereft of communities with durable relationships. And yet we
see that modernity works against us on this score, promoting
individualism, mobility, abstraction and achievement among
other things, all of which tend to weaken communal bonds and
make relationships purely voluntaristic.

For those concerned about the problem of tolerance, then, the
central question turns out to be the following: How can we
create truth-bearing communities in a modern industrial society? And, for Christians like me, who do not wish to retreat to
some kind of bucolic communalism of the past (which never
existed) or suffer under a totalitarian's prescription for a communalistic future: How can this be accomplished without creat-
ing in the process some version of the oppressive communities
that already dot the landscape of history?

Not surprisingly, many claim we can't. Some of these, of
course, are perfectly content with the current state of truthlessness and will not be persuaded regardless of the argument. But
many others have good reason to be suspicious of community,
especially those who have been the victims of communal op-
pression. Former cult members, religious martyrs, victims of
parental abuse and racism—for these the idol of tolerance may

be worth bowing down to, if only to prevent the kinds of injustices they have experienced in the past. Community, from
this vantage point, is not so much the bearer of truth but the
wielder of the whip. And so it is believed that the community's
power must be curtailed at all costs; its needs must always give
way to the needs of the individual.

From this perspective, embracing tolerance as a high value
is understandable. And I say that with more than theoretical
conviction. My own ancestors were burned at the stake in the
sixteenth century, routed in the seventeenth, forced to emigrate
to one culture in the eighteenth century and to another in the
nineteenth—all because they baptized adults rather than in-
fants and affirmed the doctrine of nonresistance. I understand
the need for forbearance.

But adopting tolerance as an end in itself—as a good, as an
ethic—is not the only way to achieve forbearance, and in the
long run it is self-defeating. For ultimately the ethic of tolerance undermines the reason for one's convictions and renders
them nonsensical. And we do not honor our ancestors by creat-
ing a society where the truths they believed are incomprehensible.

Appendix 2
Where Truth and Tolerance Endure:
A Case Study

Is it possible to have a society where there is a deep commitment to truth but where people practice tolerance toward one another's differences in belief? In one sense, if my argument up to this point holds, Christians ought to be able to respond affirmatively to that question. The truth we believe compels us to treat others justly, regardless of whether they agree with us. In other words, Christians ought to be characterized by a deep commitment to truth, and that commitment ought to produce a care and concern for others, regardless of their ideological proclivities.

But the historical reality is this: many Christians have found that objective difficult to achieve when they have seen themselves as responsible for the direction of a society. It is relatively easy to be for tolerance when one is part of a religious minority; first-century Christians had no difficulty practicing

both truth and tolerance, because they were potentially the beneficiaries of both. The real difficulty comes after a group is in a majority position, when it has become responsible for setting the laws and moral tone of a society. Christians didn't become less tolerant after Constantine because their theology had suddenly changed, but because their responsibilities and interests had shifted dramatically.

So can there be a society where *the majority* has a deep commitment to truth but practices tolerance nevertheless? Despite the difficulties, I think the answer is yes; in fact, history periodically provides us with examples of such a situation. In this chapter I want to look at just such a case, in the hope that it will help us think more clearly about this issue in our own day.

Religious Intolerance

Throughout history, the characteristic relationship between people of different religious faiths has been conflict. Religious tolerance is a far rarer species than religious intolerance. Some in the West have at times been tempted to assume that religious intolerance is simply a theological problem, an inevitable consequence of exclusivistic metaphysical claims.[1] But world history shows differently. Regardless of theological exclusivity, people of different faiths generally do battle with one another. Indeed, the primary factor in interreligious conflict appears to be not theology but hegemony.[2] Faiths that come to be regionally dominant are typically not inclined to be tolerant of minority faiths. In other words, the more pervasive a religious group's influence, the less tolerant it is likely to be. There are, of course, numerous exceptions to this rule. One appears to be the establishment of larger world empires where political authority stretches far beyond the borders of the conquering nation; in such cases a more tolerant approach is sometimes assumed to be politically expedient, as was the situation during certain periods of the Roman Empire.[3] But even in such situations tolerance is not always chosen, as various Christian and Muslim empires have repeatedly shown. And on a religious majority's home turf, political hegemony generally translates into the suppression of religious minorities.

Though this intolerance is ethically problematic, it is entirely understandable, not only sociologically but theologically as well. On the one hand, groups that gain political hegemony naturally want to extend their influence. We do not have to pick theories about why this is the case (there are many). But we ought to note that it is the rare group that gains power and does not attempt to ensure its longevity by undermining the legitimacy of its rivals.[4] That is especially true, moreover, when we come to religious conflict, precisely because the combatants assume they are not only defending a political regime but also defending orthodoxy against heresy, their deities against the gods of others. In other words, religious group conflict takes on a degree of importance that purely political conflict does not—a transcendent purpose that not only inspires the combatants but also justifies intolerance. That is why holy wars are often so brutal. And that is why every political leader wants his or her battle to be a holy war—the mother of all wars—in the eyes of the people.[5]

The point, then, is that it is entirely reasonable for people who hold strongly to their convictions to be troubled by those who hold contrary convictions, and thus the fact that religious intolerance is the modus operandi in most societies is not surprising. And it is also reasonable to expect that tolerance will exert itself most readily and with greatest ease where religious convictions are held with less fervor, less conviction.

The unusual moments in history—and the ones that ought to catch our attention—are those times when religious convictions are deeply rooted and deeply held but when tolerance is practiced nevertheless. These are the events that ought to surprise us, since, on the surface at least, they conform neither to the internal logic of metaphysical truth claims nor to the sociological logic of collective behavior.

This sort of surprise is precisely what we find in the early American experience, at times during the period of the republic's founders and almost universally when we arrive at the time of the framers of the Constitution. The question is, why?

What few would debate—and the assumption with which we can begin our answer—is that there was an unusual degree of religious tolerance that emerged in the new republic.[6] Of course this is a relative statement and must be interpreted in that light. It merely assumes that in view of the Western religious history that preceded it, the American experience in the realm of religion was marked by an unusual degree of tolerance. Certainly it would be wrong to impute modern notions of tolerance to the colonists, for, as we will see, the kind of tolerance they developed was substantially different. Similarly, we must remember that the tolerance that did emerge was selective (depending on time and place), with Protestants being far more likely to be tolerant of other Protestants than of Catholics. Nevertheless, a measure of religious tolerance did emerge, and its presence was something of a surprise, if not an anomaly. And again the question is, why?

Hypothesis: A Case of Weak Religion
One possible answer is the one developed by Alexis de Tocque-

ville, generally a source of good insight on the early American scene. It was de Tocqueville's conclusion that Americans exhibited religious tolerance in large part because there was a certain innocence, even superficiality, in the way Americans understood their own faiths.[7] His assumption was that people of different religious backgrounds tolerated one another in large measure because they didn't clearly understand the depth of their own differences or the theological implications thereof. This superficiality of conviction, he believed, allowed Americans to assume more religious commonality than there really was and to remain somewhat indifferent toward those conflicts of which they were aware. His conclusion was not intended as a disparagement of Americans, by the way, since de Tocqueville was clearly appreciative of much that he observed. Nor, for that matter, was it born out of ignorance concerning the existence of religious disagreements, since he witnessed (and took great pains to chronicle) a number of sectarian disputes, some of which were heated to say the least.[8] Rather, his appreciation of tolerance and his awareness of sectarian disputes simply made him draw his conclusion with some prudence and a modicum of wonder and amazement.

De Tocqueville's conclusion is representative of what I shall call the "weak religion" thesis, and it contains a great deal of theoretical and historical integrity. Indeed, I would argue that it was precisely the integrity of the position that compelled a good chronicler like de Tocqueville to draw it, even though he was aware of evidence to the contrary. In point of fact, tolerance typically flourishes where religious convictions wither, and conversely, tolerance dissipates when the religious turn zealous. Therefore, even though de Tocqueville (while in Michigan) "heard the Lutheran condemn the Calvinist to eternal fire and the Calvinist the Unitarian, while the Catholic embraced them all in a common condemnation,"[9] that fact was not persuasive to him. More indicative of American religion, he assumed, were the prisoners he witnessed at Sing Sing, who could attend chapel service after chapel service, each one led by a different minister with a different sectarian message, and not even know the difference.[10]

Of course there was religious indifference in early-nineteenth-century America, as there was among various peoples scattered throughout Europe at the time, as there typically is within the warp and woof of any society not in the midst of war or some other calamity. And perhaps, given the degree of pluralism that had already set in by the 1830s, it manifested itself in peculiar ways, especially to a citizen of France (the revolving door at Sing Sing being a case in point). But in the end, de Tocqueville's weak religion hypothesis fails, despite its theoretical integrity, because it simply ignores too much evidence, some of it contained in his own journals.

Frontier Americans may have held untutored convictions, but those convictions were meaty enough to carry them through the dreariest of circumstances, not to mention propel them to immigrate in the first place. More important, these folks whom de Tocqueville described were, after all, nothing more than transplanted Europeans, many of whom came to North America in the first place because of the implications of their faith. They were hardly an indifferent subgroup within Europe. And if they had become so by the early nineteenth century, a fact I will not concede, then surely it had less to do with the religiosity they brought with them than the environment they inherited on the other side of the Atlantic. In other words, if a change occurred, what produced the change?

So the weak religion thesis, though perfectly sensible in the light of religious history, hardly explains anything even if it is accurate. It certainly doesn't tell us how religious tolerance emerged in the first place. Nor does it explain its American evolutionary development, once incarnated. In spite of the credentials of its advocate, therefore, it simply will not do.

Hypothesis: A Case of Strong Religion

A second tack, and a better explanation perhaps, might be described as the "strong religion" thesis, though "strong" could be more accurately rendered "good" since there is a clear normative bent to this line of thought. This position finds its roots in a variety of different soils, but its trunk characteristic is that it views American tolerance as the product of a new kind of thinking, a new way of conceiving of the differences between religious groups. Rather than emerging out of indifference, this position argues, tolerance in early America resulted out of conviction—a growing conviction that religious tolerance was the right and moral way to handle religious diversity.

Sectarian Influence. Three forms of the strong religion thesis ought to be differentiated. In the first, the development of religious tolerance is tied directly into specific sectarian traditions, and it is argued that those traditions planted the seed that eventually flowered into a practical doctrine of tolerance. The Puritan left wing, and specifically the Quakers, for example, were early advocates of toleration, though it is not clear whether this stemmed from religious conviction or from a practical desire for freedom from persecution in seventeenth-century England. Whatever the case, William Penn's conversion to the Quaker cause and his subsequent writings about religious toleration (*The Great Case of Liberty of Conscience* in 1670 and, with Edward Byllynge, the "Concessions and Agreements" of West New Jersey), not to mention the actual institutionalization of toleration in Pennsylvania, were clearly instrumental in shaping colonial American thought about the issue.[11] Similarly, Anabaptist thought, as it developed early on among the Mennonites and the Amish in Europe and eventually came to influence Baptist groups in the Americas, was important in these debates. Especially noteworthy was the Anabaptist notion of separation of church and state, which was so prominently on display in Rhode Island and which eventually became a key component of American religious consciousness.[12]

Of course, relatively few Americans actually became Quakers or fully embraced Anabaptist thought. But the impact of such thinking is clearly visible in the documents of the new republic.

Ideological Innovation. A second form of the strong religion thesis would attribute American tolerance less to particularism and more to the general evolution of religion among the intelligentsia in the New World. In some ways this argument could be conceived of as an outgrowth of the first, except that people like Fox and Penn and Williams would have found the new thinking quite heretical. For their sake alone, we ought to keep it separate.

The basic position here is that evolving forms of American religiosity combined with imported Enlightenment ideology and domestic political needs to produce a new way of thinking about religion in America. We see that thinking in particular in Franklin and Jefferson, whose religiosity appeared almost entirely arbitrary until the last two ingredients are factored in. Franklin, for example, appeared to reduce religion to a belief in God as the Creator and Governor who rewarded good behavior and punished evil, while Jefferson was content to denude the

New Testament of all but Jesus' ethical teachings.[13] This kind
of selective religiosity makes some sense, however, when one
sees Franklin and Jefferson not as theologians attempting to
construct a new theology, but as eighteenth-century thinkers
trying to understand their world in essentially Enlightenment
terms, picking and choosing from the Christian tradition those
elements that comported (or conflicted least) with their own
intellectual commitments and at the same time served the cause
of the new nation (moral foundations in Franklin's case, individual liberties for Jefferson).

Whatever their motivations, it is clear that most of the framers of the new nation were not religiously orthodox but new-
thinking deists who used sacred symbols sparingly but strate-
gically, both in the founding documents and in their personal
lives.[14] From this, and given their political influence in the developing nation, one might conclude that the kind of religious
tolerance that emerged in America was the product of such new
thinking, the result of a novel ideological imagination.

A Common Experience. One additional form of the strong
religion thesis needs to be considered as well, one Martin Marty
described as a "republican banquet," borrowing an image from
William James.[15] Marty metaphorically describes the developing nation as a table where people of various religious view-
points are required to dine together. The act of sharing the same
table brings out their one common denominator, the fact that
they had all been the victims of religious intolerance at one time
or another in their history. Drawing on the work of Gabriel
Marcel, who argues that tolerance is really the "negation of a
negation" ("counter-intolerance," he calls it),[16] Marty envisions
religious toleration in the Americas as a reaction against the
intolerances of the past. "Forced thus to come to terms with

each other, they developed what Abraham Lincoln called 'bonds of affection' and 'mystic chords of memory' because of common experiences of a sort that were denied their ancestors."[17]

The point, then, is that something new and original did emerge on the Western side of the Atlantic, an identity born out of the intolerances of the past and a determination (and even a theology in time) to deal with spiritual differences without resorting to force. Marty makes it clear that this republican banquet emerged gradually and contentiously, and did little to diminish the level of conviction of its participants. Hot debates were a main course at this dinner table. But though the diners argued bitterly, they recognized the need to keep their arguments verbal, and in time they not only came to cherish the freedom they had cultivated, but even built it into their own religious dogmatics.

A Picnic of Necessity
Each of these angles on toleration in early America—whether perceived as a consequence of particular theological developments, syncretistic transformations or "mystic chords of memory"—clearly has a great deal of merit. Indeed, whereas one might be tempted to say that de Tocqueville forced his data to fit his theory, each of these strong religion arguments seems to build explanation upon experience and attempt to account for the whole in terms of the parts. Thus, even those who disagree with this thesis cannot dismiss the obvious impact of a Penn or a Williams, or the deistic inclinations of the framers, or the common memory of religious intolerance.

Nevertheless, as an explanation for the kind of religious tolerance that developed, the adequacy of these ideas remains in doubt. The problem is not so much in what is said but in what

is left unstated. For in each case an existential fact is taken for
an explanation, and though the fact is by all accounts accurate,
it cannot explain the uniqueness of the American religious experience.

Again, the European situation helps to clarify our thinking
at this point. All elements of the strong religion thesis were
present at various points in European history. Anabaptists early on advocated the separation of church and state: Grebel de-
nounced Zwingli's cooperation with city government at the beginning of the Reformation and set up a religious movement
explicitly rejecting such a rapprochement with the state.[18] Nevertheless, Grebel's argument was not persuasive to the majority
of Reformers, and thus the Anabaptist movement quite quickly
was marginalized and its followers persecuted as a result. Others in Europe also picked up the Anabaptist notion of church
and state, but it was decisively defeated in nearly all its incar-
nations. The question then is not where the idea came from, but
why it eventually flourished in North America but not in Europe.

The same question arises regarding the relative impact of
Enlightenment thought on both sides of the Atlantic. The
thinking of Jefferson and company was not rooted in American
soil.[19] It was the product of European intellectual developments. Nevertheless, it took a different form in North America.
Instead of being anticlerical and antichurch, it attempted to
graft itself into the tree of American religiosity, using traditional symbols where appropriate and even cooperating grandly
with the barbarians on many occasions. In other words, syn-
cretism did take place among the political intelligentsia, and it
certainly helped to contribute to religious tolerance in America.
But why did it happen on the shores of the Delaware and the

Potomac rather than the banks of the Thames or the Seine?

Finally, there is the republican banquet, which may be a proper way to describe the civil scene in America in the seventeenth and eighteenth centuries, but certainly would not characterize public life in England. But why not? The response that *there was a memory of persecution in America* is not adequate, because many of those memories were made in England and elsewhere, and had been made for some centuries prior to the immigrants' departure to the West. The point is, intolerance was not novel to the American memory. It had occurred regularly in Europe, and yet it produced only pockets of counterintolerance until far into the modern period. Why didn't the common experience of intolerance in England—with both Catholics and Protestants having ample opportunity to feel the lash of the other's whip—produce a republican banquet? Or why, in contrast, did the republican banquet come to fruition in North America in spite of the presence of a steadfast Puritanism in New England and an entrenched Church of England in Virginia?

The answer, of course, is that something very different occurred in North America, something that allowed the minority opinion on church and state in Europe to become a majority opinion in America, something that did not require anticlericalism among libertarians but encouraged cooperation instead, something that kept the memories of intolerance alive and existentially relevant, such that an ideology of freedom could take root as an American story and shape future generations. That something would later be called "pluralism" by those who use the term descriptively, but might more aptly be termed "ideological heterogeneity" (where ideology is seen to be an idea system rather than a social legitimation).

Whatever the nomenclature, the key difference between North America and Europe is that there was from the beginning a certain admixture of peoples and peoples' religions. At first, this heterogeneity was not apparent to the new arrivals. Thus the New England Puritans established their own church without regard for what was happening further south and without a thought of setting up a republican banquet, even though their collective consciousness certainly included memories of the consequences of intolerance in their mother country. The same thing could be said of Virginia, where things progressed as if the issues of pluralism were no more salient than they had been in England. But a map of North America would tell a different story, a story of increasing numbers of religious and cultural groups, and it would be the realities of the map that would shape the future.

The crucial factor in the development of religious toleration in the new country, then, was not religion, nor philosophy, nor historical memory: it was necessity.[20] This is not to say that the other factors were unimportant or to reduce the issue to a kind of geographical determinism. Had the Quaker concept of tolerance not been present in word and deed, things would have turned out differently (including the very real and logical possibility of multiple states and state religions). The same could be said for the influence of the framers, whose ability to dance with many partners—to take essentially Enlightenment notions of the individual and dress them up in ways that even the descendants of New England Puritans could stomach—was an important ingredient in the eventual outcome. The same could be said about any number of other variables without whose presence religious toleration would never have come into being. But the linchpin to it all, the thing that separates the American experience from the European, was this practical need to simply get along with others—others who owned different religious commitments and, increasingly over time, didn't live all that far away. In this sense, the American experience resembled a picnic grounds more than a banquet table, with different families each claiming their own turf, eating in relative solitude for a time, but increasingly forced to interact with other families as the popularity of the picnic area mushroomed.

The Odd Marriage

The thesis here, then, is that religious tolerance in America was in the first place a behavioral adaptation to an unusual circumstance as opposed to an ideological innovation that generated a novel form of behavior. Relatively few of those who came to the shores of North America had any intention of setting up a pluralistic arrangement when they walked across the gangplank, not even with the Native Americans who already occupied the territory. Their intention rather was to continue with the tradition of an established church, and they carried out that intention in nearly all the colonies, not only prior to the writing of the First Amendment but even for some time thereafter.[21]

Again, there were a few exceptions to this pattern, Pennsylvania being the most notable. But the relevance of these ideological exceptions is not that they led the way to a new kind of political arrangement but that they offered an alternative model when it became clear that the old one wasn't going to work. To be sure, that was no small contribution. But it would not have been accepted or considered worthy of consideration had not the practical problem of building "one out of the many" presented itself with such vigor.

The significance of this turn of events in the political arena is obvious, but we should not lose sight of its social-psychological ramifications as well. For it means that, to a large extent, Americans came to *act* on the basis of tolerance long before they came to *believe* in it—initially as a political necessity and later as a genuine good. In some ways this accounts for their ability to be so selective (or inconsistent, to put it more pejoratively) in their practice, tolerating some religious groups far more readily than others: they engaged in tolerance only to the extent that it was expedient or deemed necessary. But there is an upside to this inclination as well, especially as we compare it to the modern situation, and that is that they were not inclined to confuse tolerance with virtue, nor did tolerance undermine their commitment to the particulars of their religious faith.[22]

This odd marriage of tolerance and truth did not last forever, of course. But it did exist for a substantial length of time, and moreover, during the first few centuries of its existence the relationship actually matured considerably. One can always drive a metaphor into the ground, but if we stay within the romantic motif, we could say that in the seventeenth century truth and tolerance were not all that friendly in America, as tolerance was too young and truth was firmly established in old-style political arrangements. During the eighteenth century, however, tolerance matured considerably—out of practical necessity, remember, not grand ideals—and by the time the framers put the initial documents together to attempt a new nation, truth and tolerance had agreed to live together, if not in bliss then certainly in mutual respect. This was nothing like an egalitarian marriage, however, since truth would not have considered tolerance an equal partner but more of a necessity given other family objectives. In other words, it was a marriage of convenience.

In the nineteenth century the relationship changed somewhat, with tolerance becoming an equal partner and freedom
beginning to be treasured in American folklore as a defining
characteristic and myth. A shift was taking place, in other
words, but it was not apparent in the hearts and minds of most
Americans; the marriage appeared healthy. At the turn of the
century, however, a new pattern in the relationship clearly began to emerge, at first observable in intellectual and artsy cir-
cles but increasingly obvious in the business and familial do-
mains as well. As noted in the last chapter, this change
occurred not so much in the status of tolerance as in the health
of truth. What appeared to be minor sores and irritations in the
nineteenth century suddenly blossomed into fairly large tumors
during the early twentieth.

Parts of the body of truth continued to ignore these tumors,
acting as if nothing were wrong, while other parts were hor-
rified but assumed the problem could be cured by the simple
application of a fairly ruthless scalpel. Few people seemed to
understand that the entire body was racked with the disease,
however, except for those who were its primary carriers. True,
a segment of the carriers were worried about the final outcome
of the disease (they wrote melancholy novels, painted increasingly bizarre self-portraits and drank themselves to death), but
most said the tumors were really a sign of health, something
to celebrate rather than worry about. In the meantime, tolerance mostly lay low, not vaunting its status but putting down
roots and establishing itself as the only viable family member
(not by argumentation but by default).

By the second half of the twentieth century, however, tolerance had lost all sense of modesty or inhibition and was fully
exerting itself as the only worthy member of the family. By this

time truth was too enfeebled to resist tolerance's claims and, increasingly, in the light of those claims appeared to have no right to do so. Thus the marriage was fully dissolved, with truth taking on the role of a dying fool who is heeded only when it speaks on tolerance's behalf and whose only function is to serve as evidence of how tolerant tolerance really is.

All of the above cries out for elaboration, of course—a cry that will go unheeded for the time being. At this point, however, it is important to note that there was a place and time in Western history when tolerance and truth coexisted. It was not a time of bliss—no Camelot, certainly—but it was a period when men and women of conviction could live in relative proximity to one another yet hold on to their commitments with confidence, construct their lives according to those commitments, argue forcefully about their beliefs, have those arguments understood and countered not with accusations about intolerance but with counterarguments, and still on the whole refrain from using force as the final arbiter. And it came into being not by grand human design, but by a confluence of events and a people's practical need to live together with their disputations.

Keeping Perspective

Two points of clarification are necessary. First, it is important not to confuse my argument with those who would contend that eighteenth-century America was some kind of golden age in American or world history. That is not the contention here. My argument is limited merely to the assertion that it was a period when truth and tolerance got along in a manner that left truth intact and tolerance as the modus operandi. This argument says nothing about the adequacy of the truths that eighteenth-century Americans were committed to, for example, nor does it claim that life in general was a grand enterprise.

I actually have great difficulty with some of the truth claims of that period, some of a religious nature and quite a number of a more philosophical nature. Certainly my own commitments put me at odds with some of the assumptions of the Framers, especially regarding the nature of human reason, the place of the individual in society and the inevitability of human progress. Moreover, many of the truth claims boldly asserted in the eighteenth century were found wanting in the nineteenth and twentieth, and in some sense may be considered the progenitors of the problem of truth in our own age.

But that is not the issue here. The matter at hand is not the *content* of what was believed but the *confidence levels* of those who believed it. And my thesis is that eighteenth-century America was unusual in its ability to cultivate both robust truth commitments and a tolerant public square.

Second, it is well to highlight the oddity of the "American experiment" in those early years and therefore to remind ourselves how difficult it would be to replicate that experience. In fact, calling it an experiment seems somewhat questionable, given the generally calculative nature of the term and the essentially fortuitous quality of the tolerance that developed. It is true, of course, that eventually Americans came to appreciate the peculiarity of their situation and to think of their experience as something of a case study for the rest of the world (one thinks of Lincoln's description of Americans as God's "almost chosen people").[23] But this was pretty much an after-the-fact analysis, used to legitimate certain political objectives and to bring coherence and solidity to a society that was still prone to fragmentation. It was not the basis for the kind of tolerance that emerged in the first place. This understanding of American uniqueness, moreover, seems to be quite different from my own. Its emphasis appears to be on America's uniqueness in its tolerance, as a crucible of freedom, and in that sense as an experiment for the rest of the world. My contention is that, in hindsight, the American situation was unusual not in the measure of freedom it afforded but in the degree to which tolerance and truth coexisted. That is the genuine oddity.

This peculiar arrangement, I have also contended, was the result of a developing process in which the *act* of tolerance was generally embraced before the *idea*. Again, that is an overstatement if taken to mean that a toleration ideology was absent; certainly the idea of tolerance has quite deep roots in history, not the least of which is the exodus story among the Hebrews, whose memory led to norms of tolerance toward the alien ("Do not oppress an alien; you yourselves know how it feels to be aliens, because you were aliens in Egypt"—Ex 23:9). But that norm did not flower into a political arrangement in the West to any substantial extent until after the Protestant Reformation, and not on a truly large scale until we arrive at the American situation. The question is, Why did the idea finally take root after so many years of dormancy and neglect? The answer, I believe, is that it presented itself as the most prudent way of handling the practical problem of heterogeneity. It wasn't so much an affection for tolerance that led eighteenth-century Americans to embrace a political structure that incorporated it. Indeed, there was nothing in the way most Americans of the period lived to suggest that they thought tolerance had much existential value at all. Rather, it was determined to be the best way to handle the problem of heterogeneity, to establish some kind of unity in the face of their many differences.

Modern Implications

What the early American experience illuminates in hindsight is that the marriage of tolerance and truth is a most unlikely union. In large measure it occurred in early America by virtue of circumstance: the result of hard-boiled truth lovers meeting head-on with other hard-boiled but contrary-minded truth lovers, and stuck with the need to form a nation. It was a reluctant tolerance, in other words, grudgingly offered and grudgingly received.

But in that fact, I believe, we are offered a glimpse of what it will take to bring about such a union in the future, a glimmer of hope for those who wish to make it a fact of modern life rather than a historical peculiarity. Two assumptions must obtain to make the marriage of truth and tolerance work. First, it must be assumed that truth exists and that it is worth preserving and passing on to future generations. And second, tolerance needs to be understood not as an end but as a means, a crucial ingredient in the preservation and cultivation of truth. Under such assumptions tolerance is not something we celebrate but something that we acknowledge as a necessity in a fallen world. What we celebrate, instead, is the truth. It is truth we honor, it is truth we cherish, and it is truth on which we stake our lives.

Both assumptions are under siege in the modern world, however. Indeed, as I have already argued, modernity has managed to reverse the equation entirely, elevating tolerance to a virtue and relativizing truth in total, affirming the latter only when it promotes the goal of tolerance. Moreover, I have pointed out that this reversal makes extremely good sense, both philosophically and sociologically: it is precisely what one would expect within the context of individualism, pluralism and modernization. In such an environment, then, can we ever recover our confidence in truth, and do so without losing tolerance altogether as a means?

Truth without tolerance is a disaster of the first order, a disaster whose carnage is plainly evident on the landscape of human history. Tolerance without truth is also a disaster—though that is difficult for moderns to perceive or admit—because it undermines the very purpose and meaning of human existence; it promotes a different kind of death from intolerance, but it is a death nevertheless. So we need both, but we need them in their proper order. Is such an ordering possible in the modern world?

The question needs to be asked at two levels, I believe: at the level of the polity and at the level of the church. Politically, the question is this: Can we organize ourselves in such a way that diversity is embraced, tolerance is practiced, and truth is cultivated and cherished (by those who wish to cherish it)? The answer, I think, is yes, but it will require at least one important change in the way we organize public life: we must recognize "socializing communities" as valid entities, in and of themselves, which deserve protection and the resources to flourish. By "socializing communities" I mean primarily families, schools, churches and any other learning communities where teaching and understanding are the primary objectives. And the bottom line is that such communities must have the opportunities and resources necessary to nurture the next generation according to the truths they believe. As long as we recognize only individual rights and largely ignore the rights and responsibilities of socializing communities, we will not have truth-bearing communities. Instead we will have confused individualists without purpose or meaning in their lives and without any sense of what truth and justice entail.

For the church, though, it means something a bit different. Christians will want to work toward a more just society, on the one hand, but we will need to make sure that we have our lives in order as families, churches and communities as well. If the fundamental problem of modernity is that it undermines communities—and I think that is the case—then we will need to pay special attention to our own communal base, making sure that we act and work together as a community of believers in all these institutions. If we act as modern individualists in the midst of modernity, we are doomed. We won't value the truth. We won't teach the truth. And even if we do, few will understand it. As we act as a body, however, we need to be very careful about one thing: we must make sure that we are, in fact, the body.

I said before that American Christians have the tendency to worship with those who are like them—ethnically, economically and so on. If we approach community along those same stratified lines and our "socializing institutions" turn out to be white and middle-class, then our communities will not represent the body of Christ; they will not have all the insights and gifts of the body; and we will not wind up teaching the whole, life-changing truth of Scripture. Instead, we will more than likely act as an entrenched interest group, interested more in our own limited concerns than in the requirements of truth and justice.

And so we return to the issue that prompted this book in the first place: How do we promote both truth and justice, in these days, in these times? For Christians the answer is deceptively simple. It is the same answer for Christians in every era, in any world: We follow Jesus Christ. We believe the truth he has taught us. And that truth, when practiced, commits us to doing justice and loving mercy.

Every generation is tempted to follow other messiahs, other truths, and we are no exception. Yet within every generation are those who have been faithful to the truth of Christ in the face of great difficulties. The question is, Will we too be faithful? And will we do it . . . together?

Notes

Chapter 3: Multiculturalism

[1]James Davison Hunter, *Culture Wars: The Struggle to Define America* (New York: BasicBooks, 1991), p. 215.

Appendix 1: From Truth to Tolerance

[1]See Francis Bremer, *The Puritan Experiment: New England Society from Bradford to Edwards* (New York: St. Martin's, 1976); also Edmund Morgan, *The Puritan Dilemma: The Story of John Winthrop* (Boston: Little, Brown, 1958); Darrett Rutman, *American Puritanism: Faith and Practice* (Philadelphia: J. B. Lippincott, 1970); Virginia Anderson, *New England's Generation: The Great Migration and the Formation of Society and Culture in the 17th Century* (Cambridge, U.K.: Cambridge University Press, 1991).

[2]This usually happens in high school, and certainly by the time one arrives in college. Unfortunately, students are often set up for this reversal by the kind of one-sided view of the Pilgrims they learned as children. Having learned that the Pilgrims wanted the same kind of freedom they want, they are surprised to discover that these early Puritans were rather uncompromising when it came to questions of worldview. Consequently, there is a tendency to turn 180 degrees on the question of the Pilgrims and assume that they were heartless, loveless and ruthless. In fact, however, the Puritans of this period had a rather robust view of life and were not particularly prudish about such things as sex, drink and celebration (see Leland Ryken's *Worldly Saints* [Grand Rapids, Mich.: Zondervan, 1986]). It would be much better to start with the truth and admit to our children from the beginning that the Pilgrims were no more enamored of tolerance than they were of intolerance. A child's version that attempts to do that, by the way, is *The Pilgrims' Party: A Really Truly Story* by Sadybeth Lowitz and Anson Lowitz (New York: Stein and Day, 1959).

[3]The word *moderns* may need some clarification. By "moderns" I simply mean those who live in the modern world—modernity, for short—and that would include those whose lives are dominated by the exigencies of indus-

trial economies, growth technology and mobility. To some extent, one could say that the whole world today is dominated by such factors, but that would miss an important point: some of us are at the core of modernity (our decisions, values and education assume it) while others are at the fringes, retaining elements of traditionalism in greater or lesser amounts. Thus a person working on a farm in rural America lives in the same nation as a law professor at Yale, but the farmer's *world* is far less modern, less permeated by modern values. The literature on modernity is vast, now complicated by those who call themselves "postmodern" (some of whom mean *beyond* modernity, others a critical stance toward modernity; both are making arguments, however, that are only conceivable because of modernity). Those interested in the topic might begin with Paul Johnson's broad overview *Modern Times* (New York: Harper & Row, 1983), followed perhaps by Anthony Giddens's sociological critique in *The Consequences of Modernity* (Stanford, Calif.: Stanford University Press, 1990).

[4] I am being facetious here, of course, but only mildly so. And my point is not that "the best students of science and philosophy" necessarily have it wrong. Rather, we have traveled an interesting path with regard to truth. The modern confidence in empirical truth was born in the context of certain religious assumptions about truth. Over time, these religious assumptions became increasingly suspect while empirical claims concerning truth gained greater credence. By the time you get to the twentieth century, however, the certain foundation for even empirical truth is increasingly under attack, and today few who study science historically or philosophically believe such a foundation exists (see S. D. Gaede, *Where Gods May Dwell* [Grand Rapids, Mich.: Zondervan, 1985]). The point is, the modern world is in transition on the issue of truth, and has been for some time now. This transition is reflected especially in our conversations about religious truth, when nearly everyone couches their assumptions in tentative language. But it is increasingly seen in discussions of any form of truth, even those that were previously thought to be unimpeachable (such as science). See Alasdair MacIntyre's *After Virtue* (Notre Dame, Ind.: University of Notre Dame Press, 1984) for a discussion of the relation between truth, modernization and moral consciousness; in relation to science see Michael Polanyi's *Science, Faith and Society* (Chicago: University of Chicago Press, 1959).

[5] James Davison Hunter's work has been especially revealing in this regard, particularly his two studies of evangelicals, *Evangelicalism: The Coming Generation* (Chicago: University of Chicago Press, 1987) and *American Evangelicalism: Conservative Religion and the Quandary of Modernity* (New Brunswick, N.J.: Rutgers University Press, 1983).

[6] Understanding requires a social base, a plausibility structure (see Peter L.

Berger and Thomas Luckmann, *The Social Construction of Reality* [Garden City, N.Y.: Doubleday, 1966], pp. 92-128). It requires networks and experiences and narratives and myths, all of which give words symbolic value and meaning and make them sit deep in the belly, producing ulcers or butterflies or euphoria. And the problem of tolerance in the modern world does none of that. Thus those who risk life and limb for the sake of truth are *genuinely not understandable.*

[7]See two sections of chapter two: "Tolerance in History" and "Tolerance Today."

[8]I was first introduced to the "two revolutions" approach by Robert Nisbet (*The Sociological Tradition* [New York: BasicBooks, 1966]). His intention was to show how sociology was shaped by the multiple issues of the French and Industrial revolutions. But it struck me that by focusing on these two revolutions—the one ideological and the other socioeconomic—Nisbet had rescued social history from the twin temptations of materialism and idealism. From my vantage point, however, the issue is not that these two revolutions were equal in character or impact, or in themselves pivotal. Rather, they represent key ideological and socioeconomic trends that had great impact on the modern understanding of truth.

[9]It is my strong conviction that Christian scholars, at least, should resist the temptation to reduce history to purely ideological or material explanations. Either approach inevitably diminishes the human image, making it something less than that portrayed in God's Word. Human beings are not thoughtless victims of socioeconomic conditions, nor do they make moral and ideological decisions in a circumstantial vacuum. Rather, we are choosing, thinking, creative beings whose choices, thoughts and creations are delimited by our conditions. We do not all have the same choices, but we all choose; some have more opportunities to say yes than others, but we can all say no. Human history cannot be rightly understood, then, unless both the chooser and the conditions for choice are assumed.

[10]A good discussion of the key players in the Protestant Reformation can be found in Roland Bainton's *The Reformation of Sixteenth Century* (Boston: Beacon, 1985).

[11]John Locke, *The Reasonableness of Christianity* (1695), ed. I. T. Ramsey (Stanford, Calif.: Stanford University Press, 1958).

[12]Once it is assumed that reason—freed from tradition—operates as an honest broker, it is every thinking person's duty to root out all impediments to common sense. Tradition becomes the great evil, conspiring to thwart not only intellectual pursuits but progress as well. Commenting on the ideas that provided legitimation for the French Revolution, Robert Nisbet says: "True sovereignty, it had been argued from Hobbes to Rousseau, has its

origin in, not tradition, not the historic social authorities, but in the nature of man and in contractual assent, either actual or implicit, and it gains its majesty and its rationality from its independence of all other types of authority" *(The Sociological Tradition,* p. 116).

[13]I am thinking especially of Kant and his legacy in hermeneutics: from Schleiermacher to Hegel to Dilthey to Husserl to Heidegger and so on. But the question is also deep within British empiricism, explicitly framed by Hume. In other words, this is not simply a "German problem." It is a pivotal issue in the whole of Western thought.

[14]See Nicholas Wolterstorff's *Reason Within the Bounds of Religion* (Grand Rapids, Mich.: Eerdmans, 1976) for a concise discussion of the history and problems of foundationalism.

[15]This chronology is suggestive, not definitive. I only mean to indicate that the problem of truth does not present itself—as a problem—in the various disciplines at the same time or in the same way. Thus it was engaged much earlier in philosophy, where the question was central, than in the natural sciences, where it was assumed to be resolved in realism.

[16]The fundamental question here is, was the Industrial Revolution in the West primarily an economic necessity or a cultural consequence? The debate is old and multifaceted. Karl Marx, of course, came down decidedly on the side of economic determinism *(Capital: A Critique of Political Economy,* vol. 1 [1864; reprint New York: Random House, 1977]), and that has been more or less the argument made by those who favor world-systems theory, dependency theory or various permutations of the critical school. Max Weber *(Protestant Ethic and the Spirit of Capitalism* [1904, revised 1920; reprint New York: Macmillan, 1977]) sought to attenuate Marx's economic monism but argued that cultural factors—and specifically the value of rationalization within sectors of Protestantism—were a major ingredient in the development of bourgeois capitalism and Western industrialization. That line of thought has been followed (some say perverted) by those who argue for a more culturally inspired modernization theory today. The problem here is that Weber never intended to replace economic determinism with cultural determinism; thus some of his followers use his name in vain.

[17]A good, crisp discussion of this process can be found in "Toward a Critique of Modernity," in Peter L. Berger's *Facing Up to Modernity: Excursions in Society, Politics and Religion* (New York: BasicBooks, 1977), pp. 70-82.

[18]See Peter L. Berger, Brigitte Berger and Hansfried Kellner, *The Homeless Mind: Modernization and Consciousness* (New York: Random House, 1973).

[19]See S. D. Gaede, *Belonging* (Grand Rapids, Mich.: Zondervan, 1985).

[20]This is not a novel observation. Early on, Ferdinand Toennies picked this up in developing his distinction between modern societies and traditional

communities *(Gemeinschaft and Gesellschaft* [1887], trans. C. P. Loomis [New York: Harper & Row, 1963]). A similar distinction was made by Émile Durkheim, Max Weber and Robert Redfield, and they all noted the power of tradition in premodern societies. Though the distinctions are conceptually too simplistic, they nevertheless provide great insight into the nature of modernity. The most cogent discussion of modern character based on such contrasts, I think, remains David Riesman's *The Lonely Crowd* (New Haven, Conn.: Yale University Press, 1950); though written for the context of American culture in the fifties and sixties, it applies even more precisely today, as evidenced in Robert Bellah et al., *Habits of the Heart* (Berkeley: University of California Press, 1985).

[21]That is, we *choose* our own ideological legitimations in the modern world, and that makes them far less powerful as legitimations. For example, a young couple might justify their decision to elope to Las Vegas by employing the modern myth that they have "fallen in love." Nevertheless, it is still *their* feeling that legitimated the marriage. Thus when the feeling no longer exists, they are free to choose other modern myths (such as the necessity of self-fulfillment) to legitimate the marriage's dissolution. In other words, we moderns still use legitimations, but they have much less sticking power, precisely because we are able to use them at our own discretion.

Appendix 2: Where Truth and Tolerance Endure

[1]This especially seemed to be the assumption during the post-World War II period, when a plethora of research appeared intent upon correlating various forms of religious orthodoxy with racial and ethnic group prejudice (see, for example, Theodore W. Adorno et al., *The Authoritarian Personality* [New York: Harper & Row, 1950]; and Charles Y. Glock and Rodney Stark, *Christian Beliefs and Anti-Semitism* [New York: Harper & Row, 1966]). In hindsight, however, it is evident that most of these correlations are due to class and educational differences, with orthodoxy exerting very little independent influence on ethnic prejudice (see chapter on religion in Gardner Lindzey and Elliot Aronson, eds., *Handbook of Social Psychology,* vol. 2 [New York: Random House, 1985]).

[2]See Rodney Stark and William Bainbridge, *The Future of Religion: Secularization, Revival and Cult Formation* (Berkeley: University of California Press, 1985), especially their discussion of the influence of religious factors on Southern politics as a reflection of regional Protestant hegemony.

[3]See chapter two.

[4]In fact, the desire for power and influence seems to be the one universal assumption in nearly all theoretical approaches. Certainly, that was the case for Karl Marx *(Capital: A Critique of Political Economy,* vol. 1 [1864; reprint

New York: Random House, 1977]), who rooted class struggle in societal contradictions and assumed that the bourgeoisie couldn't help but seek greater dominance, even if in doing so they were sowing the seeds of their own destruction. Disequilibrium theories, like those of Chalmers Johnson *(Revolution and the Social System* [Stanford, Calif.: Stanford University Press, 1964]), feign to offer an alternative to the conflict model, but their self-regulating systems assume actors who pursue power as well, though they are offset by the pursuits of other actors and thus a system that seeks equilibrium. Perhaps relative deprivation theorists assume the least concerning the pursuit of power, since they take expectations as an independent variable. Here too, however, the matter in question is not whether groups seek influence—they do; the question is, when will they take collective action? (The answer is, when they feel relatively deprived.) But perhaps it is resource mobilization theory that makes the assumption of influence pursuit most starkly, by ignoring it entirely and focusing instead on how groups take advantage of opportunities and mobilize available resources; here the pursuit of power is so foundational, one can merely restrict oneself to questions of means (see Charles Tilly, *From Mobilization to Revolution* [Reading, Mass.: Addison-Wesley, 1978]).

⁵I have argued elsewhere (chapter five) that those who genuinely believe in truth ought to be the least likely to come to blows over it, since they know that truth still stands regardless of their ability to defend it. But if that is so, then why does religious conviction so often lead to conflict and intolerance? The answer is that religious conviction is not often rooted in such a high view of truth or defended by those who have truth's best interests at heart. In that sense truth is more often used than believed. And those who believe it are not those who carry out wars on truth's behalf but those who conduct their lives in the gentle confidence that it is true.

⁶Noted early on by Alexis de Tocqueville *(Democracy in America,* 2 vols. [reprint New York: Knopf, 1945) and by many others since.

⁷Alexis de Tocqueville, *Journey to America* (reprint Garden City, N.Y.: Doubleday, 1971). See also George Wilson Pierson, *Tocqueville in America* (Garden City, N.Y.: Doubleday, 1959), and Martin E. Marty, *Religion and Republic: The American Circumstance* (Boston: Beacon, 1989), to whose discussion in chap. 3 I am especially indebted.

⁸De Tocqueville, *Journey to America,* pp. 395ff.

⁹Quoted in Marty, *Religion and Republic,* p. 55.

¹⁰See Pierson, *Tocqueville in America,* p. 99.

¹¹See Edwin B. Bronner, *William Penn's "Holy Experiment": The Founding of Pennsylvania, 1682-1701* (New York: Columbia University Press, 1962); see also Alan Tully, *William Penn's Legacy: Politics and Social Structure*

in Provincial Pennsylvania, 1726-1755 (Baltimore: Johns Hopkins University Press, 1977).

[12]See Edmund S. Morgan, *Roger Williams: The Church and the State* (New York: Harcourt, 1967); see also Sydney V. James, *Colonial Rhode Island: A History* (New York: Scribner's, 1975).

[13]See Chester E. Jorgenson and Frank Luther Mott, eds., *Benjamin Franklin: Representative Selections, with Introduction, Bibliography and Notes* (New York: Hill and Wang, 1962), p. 203, and Thomas Jefferson, *Writings,* ed. Merrill D. Peterson (New York: Library of America, 1984), p. 1431.

[14]See John M. Murrin, "Religion and Politics in America from the First Settlement of the Civil War," in *Religion and American Politics: From the Colonial Period to the 1980s,* ed. Mark A. Noll (New York: Oxford University Press, 1990), pp. 28-33.

[15]Marty, *Religion and Republic,* pp. 53-76.

[16]Gabriel Marcel, *Creative Fidelity* (New York: Farrar, Strauss, Giroux, 1964), pp. 211, 214.

[17]Marty, *Religion and Republic,* p. 58.

[18]See Claus-Peter Clasen, *Anabaptism: A Social History* (Ithaca, N.Y.: Cornell University Press, 1972).

[19]I do not intend to imply here that Jefferson and his contemporaries added little novel to eighteenth-century thought; they did indeed carry the Enlightenment stream in unusual paths. Nevertheless, the wellspring for their thinking—the source that provided basic assumptions about human nature, reason and tradition, and social and political possibilities—was clearly European Enlightenment thought.

[20]This point is persuasively argued by John F. Wilson in "Religion, Government and Power in the New American Nation," in *Religion and American Politics: From the Colonial Period to the 1980s,* ed. Mark A. Noll (New York: Oxford University Press, 1990), pp. 77-91.

[21]Ibid.

[22]It is true, of course, that there were religious developments during this period which undermined Protestant orthodoxy and appeared quite "modern" in certain respects, the Unitarian movement in New England being one of the most notable. However, the impetus for these developments was not an accommodation to the modern notion of tolerance but Enlightenment thinking connected with deism. These were not attempts to deal with the sociological problem of heterogeneity, in other words, but more specifically theological attempts to deal with changing philosophical assumptions of the day. See Conrad Wright, *The Beginnings of Unitarianism in America* (Boston: Beacon, 1966).

[23]William J. Wolf, *The Almost Chosen People: A Study of the Religion of Abraham Lincoln* (Garden City, N.Y.: Doubleday, 1959).

• privatization of conviction